HONKING FOR FREEDOM

BENJAMIN J. DICHTER

WITH JOHN GODDARD

**The Trucker Convoy
That Gave Us Hope**

About the Authors

BENJAMIN J. DICHTER served as the official spokesperson for the Freedom Convoy, a sustained act of civil disobedience that inspired sister protests in thirty other countries. He is a serial entrepreneur who has graded diamonds as a certified gemologist, run a graphics store in downtown Toronto, founded his own online media company, and during the COVID-19 pandemic became the owner-operator of a long-haul rig moving freight between Canada and the United States.

JOHN GODDARD is a veteran newspaper reporter, magazine writer, and author. His books include *Last Stand of the Lubicon Cree*, which championed indigenous land rights in north-central Alberta, and *The Man with the Black Valise*, about an 1894 Ontario murder that evoked the crimes of Jack the Ripper.

Table of Contents

Unjust laws exist: shall we be content to obey them, or shall we endeavor to amend them?
— Henry David Thoreau, "Civil Disobedience"

Chapter 1

Enemy of the State

My lawyer told me to leave town immediately. The police could arrest me, the bail judge could ban me from protesting, and if that happens who will go out there and speak for freedom? I told him to stop being dramatic. Nobody is going to kick down the door and cuff me.

"They might," he said.

All morning, from our respective hotel rooms, we were getting updates on the police crackdown. The prime minister had invoked the Emergencies Act, authorizing police powers normally reserved for war or national insurrection to crush one of the most peaceful, most problem-free mass political demonstrations in the country's history. Out my window I could see rooftops freshly covered by an overnight snowfall, as picturesque as a Christmas card, but three blocks away lines of police officers from multiple jurisdictions were taking up position dressed in sleek, black, riot suits.

Somebody rapped on my door. When I opened it, ten people rushed in, all from the remaining core leadership team. "The cops pulled their guns on one of the truckers last night," one of them said. "They smashed the windows and dragged him into the snow."

Everybody was looking at me. Two organizers had also been arrested the night before. "What are you thinking?" I said. "I'll support whatever you decide."

"Maybe it's time to leave," someone said.

"I agree, it's time we got out," said somebody else.

Others nodded.

"Can you put out the message?"

We had grown from a small protest group to a mass grassroots movement. We knew that some demonstrators would go but others would "hold the line," confident that if they remained peaceful they would not be harmed. Team members relayed our decision to various police liaison officers, and I posted bulletins to social media.

"It's time to leave," I wrote at 11:58 on various platforms. "@OttawaPolice, please allow the remaining trucks to leave in #Peace."

An hour later, somebody came by to say the police were advancing. Nobody in the crowd was throwing rocks, or wearing a disguise, or doing anything to make trouble. People were simply standing their ground. Some were chanting "peace, peace, peace." The officers faced them in a solid line, shoulder-to-shoulder, forming a wall. They took two or three small steps, paused, and stepped forward again, methodically, relentlessly. They wore helmets and visors. They carried hardwood batons, pepper-spray launchers, and what they called "non-lethal mid-range impact weapons," designed to stagger and injure but not kill.

"BREAKING," I wrote at 1 p.m. "Ottawa police are now boxing in 'protestors' and executing mass arrests."

I kept thinking I was safe. Two weeks earlier, I had slipped on the ice and snapped my right ankle. Half my leg was in a cast, and, except for hobbling to nearby meetings or to Parliament Hill to make a speech, I was mostly confined to the media suite at the Sheraton Hotel. As police pressed forward, however, I wondered if the lawyer might be right. When word came that a mounted unit was forming in front of the Senate Building, on oversized horses wearing plexiglass visors, I started to pack.

The problem was how to get out. Police had cordoned off a large parcel of downtown that they called "the Red Zone." To control access they were manning 100 checkpoints. Nobody could enter without papers to prove they lived or worked in the area, or had some other good reason to be there. I called a friend in the suburbs to say I was coming and ordered an Uber. It took a while. On the app, I watched the car progress in fits and starts, negotiating one checkpoint, then another. When it got close, a colleague carried my suitcase downstairs and somebody else held on to me as I walked to the curb, not letting me slip again. A green Toyota Corolla pulled up. Awkwardly, I lowered myself backward into the rear seat, stowed my crutches one at a time, and I was away.

Almost nothing else downtown was moving. The streets were nearly empty. I could have been riding through Beirut after curfew, if Beirut were ever covered in ice and snow. Every few blocks, we passed a police car with a couple of officers standing and looking around. I felt self-conscious, maybe a little paranoid, and pulled my parka hood over my head. Eventually, we reached the ramp to the Queensway, the southern boundary of the Red

Zone, and saw cars backed up more than a kilometre trying to get into the city.

I made it to my friend's building and shuffled to the entrance. Our plan had been for me to come on Monday, when she would help me with follow-up appointments for my ankle, and I was three days early. The least I could do was pay for dinner. We decided on Greek souvlaki, but when I clicked "checkout" on the Uber Eats app I got a pop-up alert: "Insufficient funds, please check your credit card balance." Paying the taxi hadn't been a problem. I tried a second time, then a third.

I felt like Will Smith in *Enemy of the State* when his card is declined at the hotel desk. "Maybe you forgot to initialize it," the clerk says. "Run this one, please," Will says, and when his second card doesn't go through he knows what's happening. He knows that Jon Voight has frozen his cards and bank accounts to block him from exposing a deep-state plot to expand surveillance over the entire domestic U.S. population. On my phone, I checked my bank accounts — corporate and personal. Both were frozen. Both transaction histories were wiped clean.

"What's the matter?" my friend said.

"Looks like they did it."

"No."

Under the Emergencies Act, citing "terrorist financing," Canadian Finance Minister Chrystia Freeland said she would freeze bank accounts to defund and disperse the Freedom Convoy. She would order financial institutions to target individual leaders and truckers protesting the government's coercive COVID-19 vaccine mandates and, if necessary, also order them to freeze the accounts of tens of thousands of participants and anybody else who contributed to crowdfunding campaigns that had twice topped $10 million in small donations. She would impose financial penalties so extreme that no Western democracy had ever used them against political demonstrators, let alone non-violent ones.

My friend was upset. I tried to calm her.

"It's going to work out," I said. "Give it time. This is too stupid to last."

Chapter 2

Convoy to End the Mandates

Brigitte Belton went on TikTok while stopped for the night in northeast Alabama. She was hauling chemicals from Georgia to a sawmill near High Level, Alberta, a journey of more than 4,500 kilometres (2,800 miles). She was feeling low. In two weeks, the Canadian government would for the first time make vaccination against COVID-19 mandatory for truckers entering or re-entering Canada, and she wasn't vaccinated.

Hauling freight to and from the United States was how Belton made her living. She was fifty-two years old, married to another trucker in Wallaceburg, Ontario, halfway between Sarnia and Windsor, near the U.S. border. To continue working, she would have to do what the government told her, but she distrusted the vaccines. She had no objection to other people taking them — she was not anti-vax — but she viewed COVID-19 vaccines as experimental and rushed to market and felt strongly about her right to bodily autonomy, her right to choose for herself whether to take the shots or not. For weeks, she had been airing her troubles on TikTok and had struck up a correspondence with "BigRed," a western-Canadian trucker she had never met. Together, they had begun to discuss the idea of a protest. Sitting in her cab in northeast Alabama, two hours into New Year's Day 2022, she posted her latest thoughts almost as a manifesto.

"Convoy to End the Mandates," the subject heading read. "We're getting ready together to fight for our freedoms, vaccinated or unvaccinated, against lockdowns and overreaching government mandates. This won't stop until we say 'No more.'"

Over the next few days on the drive north, Belton fleshed out the idea in her head. The protest wouldn't be a single convoy. In every province and state along the Canada-U.S. border, in every city and town that had a commercial trucking company or companies, drivers would form a local convoy and execute what she called a "slow roll." The vehicles would drive in a line, more slowly than usual, to attract attention and delay the delivery of goods on which the country depended. They wouldn't block roads. They wouldn't block bridges. They wouldn't do anything illegal. They would slow-roll until federal authorities acknowledged their grievances.

Partly, Belton borrowed the idea from a work disruption a few months earlier at the Canada Border Service Agency. Unionized employees, after more than three years without a contract, staged a "work to rule" strike at airports, land borders, and commercial shipping ports, causing long lineups and lengthy waits for truckers like Belton and everybody else. Federal authorities got the message. Within thirty-six hours, the government signed a new contract with the union.

The "Convoy to End the Mandates" would bring a similarly quick result, Belton told her followers. BigRed promoted the idea to his large social-media following. A trucker named "Barracuda Barbie" put them in touch with Colin Valentim in Savona, B.C., who spread the word throughout the west coast. The network kept expanding, and on January 11, from northern Texas, Belton publicly formalized the slow-rolling-convoys idea.

"This isn't just for truckers," she told her TikTok listeners. "We're in the big vehicles, and everybody is going to see us, but it's not just about us. This is for every last person who's been affected by the mandates."

She attached a photo, not of a truck but of people from different occupations — truckers, nurses, civil servants, construction workers, airline attendants, police officers, and others who faced layoff or firing for lack of one or two vaccinations. In the post, Belton also listed seven regional volunteer road captains. Valentim would organize slow-rolls in British Columbia. BigRed would co-ordinate southern Saskatchewan. Belton herself would lead drivers in the Sarnia area, at the international border. Others would register drivers and map out routes in other regions.

The response came almost instantly, or as Belton puts it, "My email box was going absolutely insane." Messages poured in from as far away as Newfoundland, Nunavut, and Washington State. From Edmonton a CBC reporter called.

"I will not get the shot in the arm," Belton told him. "Who am I really protecting? I live in my truck. When I go home, I go home to my husband, who's also a truck driver."

Why the new rule was being imposed on cross-border truckers now, the federal government never made clear. For nearly two years, truckers were getting vaccinated at a rate equivalent to the rest of the population but had remained exempt from compulsory immunization. Prime Minister Justin Trudeau deemed trucking an essential service and went out of his way to praise truckers for the risks they took to deliver necessities.

"While many of us are working from home, there are others who aren't able to do that — like the truck drivers who are working day and night to make sure our shelves are stocked," he posted to Twitter. "So when you can, please #ThankATrucker for everything they're doing and help them however you can."

The first federal travel restrictions in Canada were imposed on air passengers. In November 2020, a few months into the pandemic, the government introduced a digital vaccine passport, ArriveCAN, and required all air travellers arriving or transiting in Canada to download it to their phone. Prior to boarding a flight to Canada, passengers had to use the app to register their contact information, travel details, and proof of at least two vaccinations. They also had to state which vaccines they had received, and when, and in which country or countries.

Three months later, in February 2021, the government extended the mandate to land travellers into Canada, except truckers. Nine months after that, the government announced it would remove the exemption.

As of January 15, 2022, commercial truck drivers entering Canada would be required to submit proof-of-vaccination details either into an ArriveCAN app on their phone or into a government ArriveCAN website. Unvaccinated U.S. truckers would automatically be refused entry. Canadian truckers could not be blocked from their own country, but without submitting ArriveCAN data they would face overwhelming, almost sadistic, new barriers. Without exception, they would be required to take a COVID-19 molecular test within seventy-two hours of reaching the border, take a second test at the border, take a third test eight days after arriving in Canada, and — no matter what the test results — be required to quarantine for fourteen days. A molecular test in the United States cost up to CAN$200 at the time, and after three consecutive negative tests, a trucker would still be grounded for two weeks. In addition, Canadian border officials could decide at their own discretion whether to order a trucker to go into quarantine right away or after they delivered their load. The mandate was designed to kill the job of any unvaccinated cross-border Canadian trucker.

No incidents of truckers spreading the disease had been reported. No new scientific data had come to light. Infections, hospitalizations, and deaths were sharply down generally in Canada, and vaccine mandates were being lifted in a number of European countries. The new cross-border vaccine mandate appeared to be a solution without a problem.

"An unnecessary federal government policy," said Saskatchewan Premier Scott Moe.

"Show us the data that this mandate for truckers is necessary — we've seen nothing so far," said Saskatchewan Conservative MP Warren Steinley.

"They were heroes and now all of a sudden they are not to be trusted — I don't understand," said Barry Prentice, a transportation economist at the University of Manitoba.

Other critics warned of economic harm.

Canada is "facing a critical supply-chain crunch," said Alberta Premier Jason Kenney. "Ottawa is making a bad situation much worse."

"Maybe they don't care about nectarines or peaches or grapes," said Sandro Saragiotto, president of Offshore Canada Logistics Inc., a Toronto transportation company specializing in perishables.

"If you walk into a grocery store and you see products on the shelves, thank a trucker," said federal Conservative Finance Critic Pierre Poilievre. "If you walk into a grocery store and see empty shelves, thank Justin Trudeau."

The Canadian Trucking Alliance estimated the new ArriveCAN mandate would sideline 12,000 cross-border Canadian truckers, aggravating supply-chain issues and a driver shortage. At the same time, the alliance stated that it opposed protests on public roadways, highways, and bridges.

On January 12, three days before the cross-border rule was to take effect, Belton received a message through a trucking group to call James Bauder in Calgary, Alberta. Bauder was not a trucker. He was an activist and gadfly who, three years earlier in his motorhome, had joined a convoy of 170 vehicles to Ottawa called "United We Roll," a protest against federal energy policy. Now, he told Belton, he was organizing his second attempt at something he called "Operation Bear Hug." He would lead a convoy to Ottawa to demand an end to all federal, provincial, and municipal vaccine mandates, vaccine passport requirements, and COVID-19-related fines. If the government refused, he would replace the government. He, the governor general, and the Senate would govern the country instead of the prime minister and House of Commons, a plan laid out in a six-page "Memorandum of Understanding." To Belton, he proposed to lead a combined Convoy to End the Mandates/Operation Bear Hug, arriving in Ottawa on February 14.

"Honey, you can't do this," she told him. "For one thing, your dates are all wrong." The Convoy to End the Mandates would be leaving sooner.

The next day, January 13, Belton and Bauder convened a Facebook Live meeting with several others. It was a mismatched crew. Among them was BigRed, whose real name is Chris Barber, a six-foot-four trucker and trucking-company owner in Swift Current, Saskatchewan. Two of his regional captains were included on the call. A friend of Bauder's named Pat King, from Red Deer, Alberta, also participated. Like Bauder, King was not a trucker, but a self-styled social-media personality and loose cannon.

For the group, Bauder revised his pitch. He dropped the "Operation Bear Hug" label and February arrival date, but pushed ahead with the idea of going to Ottawa. The "Convoy to End the Mandates" should not be a synchronized collection of local slow-rolls, he said. It should be a rollout of convoys from every part of the country, converging on the Parliament Buildings and the Prime Minister's Office. He had worked out trucking routes, he said. He had maps that everybody could download.

"I'm in," a couple of people said.

Nobody raised strong objections.

"I guess we're going to Ottawa," Belton said.

The protest would be called "Freedom Convoy 2022," not as precise as "Convoy to End the Mandates" but bolder, catchier. It would send a single message — end the ArriveCAN app and all other COVID-19 mandates.

"We're all sick of mandates and we all want to stop them," Belton told the group, emphasizing for Bauder and King the convoy's focused objective. "We are not driving to Ottawa to bring down the government. We're not driving there to demand Trudeau's resignation or anything else. We are going there to end the mandates. If you have any other reason for going, you need to drop out."

The next day, Tamara Lich (pronounced Leach), came on the scene. More than any other single participant, she was to become the convoy's public face, Canada's most visible leader against the pandemic restrictions. She was forty-nine years old, married with a family, and living in Medicine Hat, Alberta. She worked in an administrative position for an oil company, and knew scores of people from various pro-oil-and-gas and anti-carbon-tax demonstrations. Her parents owned a pilot-truck company, escorting vehicles with wide, heavy loads. Hearing about the convoy, she got in touch with Chris Barber and offered to start a "Freedom Convoy 2022" Facebook page and a GoFundMe campaign. She would raise food-and-fuel money for the trip, she said, with a goal of $20,000.

The fundraising page displayed Lich's name, one reason for her eventual prominence. Another reason was her personal magnetism. She possesses an unusual warmth. When she is speaking with somebody, she offers her full attention and presence, as though nothing else around her exists. She also shows her emotions. All the way to Ottawa, riding in BigRed's semi, she would soon be posting videos of herself giving tearful reactions to what she was seeing, hearing, and experiencing. As the convoy's most identifiable figure, she would also become the Trudeau government's No. 1 political target, subjected to abuse from the police and the judicial system.

At the Facebook Live meeting, Belton set the arrival date in Ottawa as Friday, January 28. The date was symbolic, she said. On that day in 1986, the Space Shuttle Challenger exploded shortly after liftoff killing the seven astronauts aboard. "Science isn't perfect, it's flawed," she said of the lesson she took from the disaster.

Somehow Bauder wasn't paying attention. On his website, where people were going for maps, he announced the Ottawa arrival date as Saturday, January 29, 2022, which became the official date. If the convoy was as successful as the Canada Border Service Agency work-to-rule action, the leaders told each other, Trudeau would drop federal vaccine mandates within thirty-six hours of the mass arrival. If he took longer to respond, the trucks would stay longer. They would stay in Ottawa, the organizers said, "for as long as it takes."

Chapter 3

Tamara Lich Calls

My driver's licence identifies me as Benjamin J. Dichter, but on social media I use BJ Dichter, because it's shorter. Some people call me Benjamin. Some call me BJ. I live on an upper floor of a high-rise apartment building in midtown Toronto and work at a computer desk against a large, front window that offers a bird's-eye view of the neighbourhood. On the morning of January 18, 2022, I could see a snowplow making its way noiselessly up the street. Thin columns of steam rose from roof vents in the houses spread out below. I was quietly editing a podcast when the phone rang.

"Benjamin, I need your help." It was Tamara Lich. We had met in Alberta two years earlier and liked to keep in touch. "The cross-border vaccine passport just kicked in," she said. "A bunch of us want to drive to Ottawa in a convoy."

"Okay."

"I started a GoFundMe. The first day we raised $30,000. That was four days ago. We just hit $200,000."

"Hey, that's great."

"The thing's exploding," she said, sounding a little anxious. "People are sending money. Truckers are signing up from everywhere. I need you to speak for us. I love these truckers, I love these guys, but I'm worried about them saying the wrong thing. I need somebody to communicate effectively with the media, somebody assertive but careful. We don't want to incite any problems. I also want you to look over a press release I drafted. Can you do that?"

"Sure. You know I have a truck?"

"Get out."

"Yeah."

"A pickup?"

"No, no, I'm serious. I've got a Volvo VNL 670 semi. It's a part-time thing. My brother and I do runs to Connecticut and Pennsylvania."

"Fucking-A. I'm sending the release. Have a look."

I didn't even need to think about it. I had no idea how much time the convoy might take, or that it would morph into one of the biggest political protests in Canadian history and change my life, but I was fed up with more and more restrictions that made less and less sense. I'm not anti-vax. I was fully vaccinated. I even take the flu shot every year. I've never been nervous of the COVID-19 vaccines, but I support a person's right to decide for themselves whether to take them. Everybody has a right to physical autonomy.

The problem for me, being a techie, was the digital vaccine passport. Years ago, when I went to Brazil, I had to show a little yellow booklet at the airport to prove I had been immunized against certain diseases. I didn't like it but I showed it. The

ArriveCAN app is completely different. It's dangerous. It uses a QR code, a quick-response digital code, which can be used as a tracking device. It runs on the same platform as the Chinese social-credit surveillance system. Everybody complains about Facebook's or Instagram's terms and conditions, but at least with Facebook and Instagram you can opt out. With the government, you can't opt out unless you move to another country.

In early 2021, a UK research firm reported that the ArriveCAN app could give the Canadian government access to a user's location data. The Canadian health department replied that it would not use the data. "Access to the GPS location would need explicit permission from the user," the department said, a denial that left open the possibility that, if government policy changed, the app could indeed be used as a tracker.

I looked through Tamara's news release and posted it to the GoFundMe page. She named me as co-organizer and convoy spokesperson.

"Our current government is implementing rules and mandates that are destroying the foundation of our businesses, industries and livelihoods," the statement read. "We are taking our fight to the doorsteps of our Federal Government and demanding that they cease all mandates…. It is imperative that this happens because if we don't our country will no longer be the country we have come to love."

At the same time, Trudeau was digging in. When asked by a reporter about the potential economic harm from the cross-border trucking mandate, he said the United States would soon impose a matching regulation and "we are aligned with them." An alarming television interview also surfaced. A few weeks earlier, on the Quebec show *La Semaine des 4 Julie*, Trudeau expressed something close to hatred of anybody objecting to COVID-19 vaccines. He didn't attack the Freedom Convoy — it hadn't yet formed — but he vilified anybody who advocated that mandates be dropped and that an individual has a right to choose.

"We are going to end this pandemic by proceeding with vaccination," he told a studio audience in French. "There are also people who are fiercely against vaccination, who don't believe in science. They're often misogynists, also often racists. It's a small group that muscles in, and we — as a leader and as a country — have to make a choice: Do we tolerate these people?"

In response, Tamara and I developed two guiding principles for the convoy. First, no matter how much some of us might resent Trudeau's hostility, the convoy would not align itself with an opposition party. The People's Party of Canada would likely try to woo us. The Conservative Party of Canada might attempt to co-opt us. The independent member of the Ontario legislature, Randy Hillier, would almost certainly try to latch onto us. No matter what, we would remain unaligned and nonpartisan, unamenable to anybody's external political agenda. Second, we would stay in Ottawa until we got results. As the original organizers pledged, we would stay until we saw evidence that our demands were heard and understood. If the police tried to remove us, we would hold the line.

Chapter 4

The Trucks Start to Roll

Days before the trucks set out, B.C. organizer Colin Valentim posted a video that established the tone for the entire cross-country venture. At the wheel of his rig, engine chugging in the background, he faced the camera dressed in a checked shirt, dark jacket, high-visibility vest, and a black baseball cap with red trim. He delivered no impassioned speech, uttered no rallying cry. Instead, he spoke in a calm, measured tone from someplace deep and still within him, encouraging people of every description to join the national project.

"We are specifically looking to this convoy to be as loud and as large as possible, with as many people," he said in his composed way. "If you can't drive, be on the overpasses. If you can drive — cars, vans, pickups, RVs, bobtail trucks, everything we can get, anything we can get — be as loud and as visible as possible. We do not want to block roads. We're just going to continue down in the right-hand lane, doing our thing, making our miles…. Join from any part, from any location. Leave from any part or any location. It doesn't really matter. People who can go all the way east, we welcome you. If you can only go twenty blocks, we welcome you. We just need people. We need to show this government that what they're doing is wrong, and that we just won't take it anymore."

His words were like a spark to dry tinder. For two years, people had followed the instructions of the public health authorities. People had rallied to "flatten the curve." They had stayed home during lockdowns except to get groceries. They had worn a mask over their mouth and nose, shuttered their business, confined their travel to within their own region, restricted their social life to their own bubble, and, at a rate exceeding that of almost every other country in the world, rolled up their sleeve to get vaccinated. They had done what was asked and expected of them, but, after two years, the rules were making less and less sense, and no political party — federal or provincial — was raising an objection. Debate was almost non-existent. White-collar workers could continue to work from home and even save money on transit and dry-cleaning bills, but tradespeople and small-business owners, despite subsidy programs, were left at a stark disadvantage. Nobody was speaking for them. In the legislatures and in the media, nobody would discuss risk versus reward, physical health versus mental health. Individuals were left to feel guilty and alone. Anybody with doubts was left to feel ashamed for wanting their life back, or for wanting to live in a way that at least took into account individual risk-tolerance based on age and level of wellbeing. Then, without giving a reason, just as the Omicron variant was proving weaker than its predecessors, and at a time when other countries were dropping vaccine passports and other restrictions, Prime Minister Trudeau ordered cross-border truckers to download the ArriveCAN app and get vaccinated or lose their jobs, no exceptions.

That was it, the last straw. Enough was enough. "This won't stop until we say 'No more,'" Brigitte Belton posted to TikTok. "We just won't take it anymore," Colin Valentim told his YouTube audience. The self-reliant truckers broke the trance. They shattered the illusion of conformity, smashed the false narrative of unanimity. They climbed into their large, powerful vehicles to drive as many as 5,000 kilometres (3,100 miles) to Ottawa and invited like-minded people throughout the country to join them, in whatever way they could.

On Saturday, January 22, at seven in the morning, the first convoy left Prince Rupert, 750 kilometres north of Vancouver. GoFundMe donations surpassed $1.1 million. A few big rigs mingled with cement trucks, cargo vans, pickups, SUVs, and ordinary family cars. Collecting vehicles as it went, the fleet honked its way up Highway 16 through Terrace, Smithers, Houston, Fraser Lake, and Vanderhoof, cheered in every town and village by lines of people holding placards and waving Canadian flags. At Prince George, the first overnight stop, hundreds of people came to welcome the convoy with hot food, drinks, and hugs for the drivers, a scene to be repeated night after night at every staging area right across the country.

"This isn't about a vaccine, it's about a vax mandate," said Pamela Rouse, a woman with dark, curly hair from Prince Rupert who had joined the convoy in her family car. "The only thing I had to hear on the news one day... was some prime minister who's supposed to be running this country call me a misogynist, and every other woman behind me that's supporting their family....

I'm not going to let this go down without telling every single Canadian that this is not right, and this is not who we are."

The next day, Sunday, scores of big rigs — horns honking, emergency lights flashing — rolled out of the pre-dawn fog in the community of Delta, south of Vancouver. In a long procession, they moved onto Highway 1, the Trans-Canada Highway, with 4,500 kilometres of pavement ahead, and, as they drove, dozens more trucks merged with them coming off ferries from Vancouver Island and highways from the B.C. interior.

GoFundMe donations surpassed $2.2 million. Videos appeared on social media. They showed animated crowds lining the route and screaming over the honking horns. Everybody seemed to know what to do. People from Langley cheered from the 200th Street overpass. People in Aldergrove waved and shouted from the 264th Street overpass. At Abbotsford, the first big town, hundreds of people jammed the McCallum Road overpass waving Canadian flags and home-made posters saying, "No Forced Vax" and "No Truckers, No Food." As the day progressed, the numbers multiplied. Boisterous throngs turned out in Chilliwack, Hope, Kamloops, Salmon Arm, Revelstoke, and Golden.

The crowds looked like those that come out for Canada Day, or a Royal Tour, except that Canada Day falls on July 1 and Royal Family members usually visit in the summertime. Convoy supporters wore scarves, toques, and heavy mitts, and cheered above the horns as though from the stands of a hockey rink. At every location, they waved the Maple Leaf flag and sang "O Canada," which for them doubled as an anthem about freedom and uniting against threats to Canadian liberty. "True north strong and free," they sang. "Glorious and free." "We stand on guard for thee." They also held up hand-drawn posters reading, "Mandate

Freedom," "Thank You Truckers," "Let Freedom Roll," and, more sharply, "Truck You Fudeau."

On Monday, donations surpassed $3.5 million. The line of trucks gathered strength. At an overnight stop in southeast Calgary, more than 1,000 people congregated to welcome the columns arriving from southern British Columbia and from the north via Edmonton. At the next stop in Medicine Hat, Tamara Lich climbed into Chris "BigRed" Barber's semi as hundreds of supporters swarmed the rig to wish them well.

At Regina, trucks approached from the north and west, like tributaries flowing into the main channel. Drivers who wished to stay local circled the city on a slow-roll. Those joining the national motorcade continued east along the Trans-Canada. At several spots, mobs of well-wishers gathered to greet them, including former federal Conservative Leader Andrew Scheer. "No one should lose their job for a healthcare decision," he said of people choosing not to be vaccinated.

On Tuesday, the trucks continued eastward through Saskatchewan and Manitoba. The excitement followed them like a wave. Donations surpassed $4 million. Tannor O'Krane, who joined the convoy in Alberta in his car, posted videos to his YouTube channel, "Tireroaster's Garage," including some of the first drone footage showing lines of trucks stretching to the horizon. Facebook support groups formed, drawing tens of thousands of members, and from the roadsides and overpasses people of all ages, including small children, again waved flags and homemade placards. At night, supporters lit bonfires and set off fireworks.

"A great day," said Marilyn Ostash, waving from the side of a service road for an hour and fifteen minutes, as trucks filed past Brandon, Manitoba.

"I'm here to support the truckers because I think mandates are stupid," said Melanie Sawatzky, a supporter from Steinbach, southwest of Winnipeg.

"These mandates have created division," said Jolene Conway from St. Malo, south of Winnipeg. "This shows that everybody is coming together — the vaxxed, the unvaxxed, doesn't matter."

Everybody had a story to tell. Women from several Hutterite colonies cooked an immense amount of food, including four roasted pigs, to serve drivers at a stop in Headingley, outside Winnipeg. When they couldn't get near the place for the crowds, they drove two and a half hours into Ontario and had food ready for the truckers when they arrived in Kenora.

On Wednesday morning GoFundMe contributions surpassed $5.3 million. "We thank you all for your donations," Tamara wrote on the webpage, "and know that you are helping reshape this once beautiful country back to the way it was."

At the Manitoba-Ontario border, an unmarked Ontario Provincial Police cruiser met Chris Barber's Saskatchewan convoy and offered a 2,000-kilometre escort to Ottawa. "I was on the phone with them the whole way — full communications," Barber said later. "Hats off to them."

On Thursday morning donations surpassed $6.3 million. Facing a bitter wind, hundreds of people flourished flags and signs from a Highway 401 overpass outside London, Ontario, and at the next interchange an excited throng greeted scores of rigs pulling into the Flying J truck stop. Two convoys merged there. One came from Windsor. The other, of nearly a hundred vehicles, including many cars, arrived from Sarnia led by Brigitte Belton.

Chapter 5

Two Freedom Convoys

"Absolutely incredible," Krista Ford Haynes posted to Instagram from an overpass near Milton, in the western outskirts of Greater Toronto. She had made herself one of the province's harshest critics of COVID-19 mandates after her husband, David Haynes, had been laid off from the Toronto Police Service, without pay, for not getting vaccinated. She was also the eldest daughter of Ontario Premier Doug Ford, who had imposed the mandates.

"Today was a damn good day," she wrote with the enthusiasm typical of people witnessing the trucks and the crowds. "I had a moment to walk to the bottom of the bridge to look up and simply admire the hundreds of beautiful faces that showed up to stand for our freedoms, a moment I wanted to soak in and engrave as a memory. It was so beautiful to watch everyone come together and unite. From strollers to walkers, all different races and religions coming together to keep our freedoms. There is nothing more electric and powerful than we the people uniting under one house."

Elsewhere on the city's western outskirts, Brigitte Belton's Windsor-Sarnia column merged with a line of vehicles from Fort Erie and Niagara. Some drivers were slow-rolling locally. Others were joining the convoy to Ottawa. From one end of the urban expanse to the other, in a piercing wind and sometimes driving snow, countless thousands of people, maybe tens of thousands, lined portions of the route and crammed bridges. They waved flags from hockey sticks and from between snowshoes and held up giant Valentine's hearts.

East of Toronto, Belton stopped briefly at a rally in Port Hope, where supporters served hot dinners and distributed bottled water, soft drinks, and bag lunches. In Napanee, between Belleville and Kingston, she stopped again at a Flying J, this time accepting a meal of chili, baked potatoes, and chicken wings, served outdoors in minus twenty degrees. Women offered her food to take with her, but her seats were already full from the London stop.

"What can we give truckers other than dinners and bag lunches?" volunteers would ask.

"Get your kids involved," Belton would say, repeating an idea she was promoting online.

"What do you mean?"

"Get your three-year-old to draw a picture and give it to a trucker."

"Are you kidding me?"

"No, we're doing this for us, but we're doing it for our kids, too. Get them involved. Draw us pictures. These might look like the biggest, baddest guys you'd ever want to meet, but put a kid in front of them and they're marshmallows."

Drawing pictures became as big a part of Freedom Convoy involvement as waving a flag or singing "O Canada." Often under the title "Thank You Truckers" or "We Love You Truckers," children would draw either directly on a lunch bag or on a separate piece of paper tucked inside a bag. Sometimes, a parent would give the child a boost up to a truck window, and the child would hand the picture directly to the driver.

On Friday morning, beacon flashing from her roof, Belton led the southern Ontario fleet up Highway 416 into the nation's capital. As the trucks approached downtown, electronic billboards instructed them to exit at Pinecrest Road and take the Sir John A. Macdonald Parkway to the Canadian War Museum parking lot, walking distance from Parliament Hill. Once everybody was settled, Belton left for Arnprior, sixty kilometres (thirty-seven miles) away, to guide a northern Ontario convoy into the city. The next day, she would to do the same for Chris Barber and his Saskatchewan contingent. When parked, his convoy filled two truck-stop lots and a farmer's field. On the highway it extended twelve kilometres (seven and a half miles).

Trucks were also coming from the east coast. At around the time Belton left Sarnia on Thursday, a legion of Newfoundlanders and Maritimers pulled out of the Big Stop at Enfield, Nova Scotia, north of Halifax. It was a frosty morning. Hundreds of supporters, including parents with children, cheered the departure, again with flags wrapped across shoulders and flying from hockey sticks. The procession crossed New Brunswick, cheered by more crowds from bridges and roadsides, and at the St. Lawrence River, at Rivière-du-Loup, the trucks turned west toward Quebec City and Montreal.

On Friday morning, smaller fleets formed at towns along the U.S. border and rolled across Quebec's Eastern Townships to meet the main flow at Montreal's western suburbs. Festive, patriotic crowds appeared. Quebec and U.S. flags flew with Canadian ones, and on Highway 40, part of the Trans-Canada, countless ordinary motorists joined the noisy celebration. In a single strip, as far as the eye could see, hundreds of vehicles mingled with the rigs, clogging the right-hand lane to a near standstill, while leaving the passing lane free for other traffic.

Slowly, the line snaked into Ontario. For the long-haulers, the destination was Herb's Travel Plaza, a stop outside Vankleek Hill, one hour from Ottawa. It would be their overnight staging area for the final Saturday-morning push to the capital. The parking lot was huge but not huge enough. Giant, yellow snowplows arrived to clear the frozen, surrounding fields, creating a massive surface as hard as asphalt. The trucks parked, and the countdown to the final morning cavalcade began.

Anybody tuning in to CBC Radio that Friday — the day before the official arrival at Parliament Hill — would have had no clue about the excitement and exhilaration sweeping the country. "The Media is the Virus," some placards said along the way, but no criticism fully captured the extremes of the state broadcaster's willful blindness.

The Current, CBC Radio's morning newsmagazine, buried the convoy story. Host Matt Galloway opened with a COVID-19 update from Dr. Bonnie Henry, B.C.'s chief medical officer of health, the type of interview he had been conducting for two years. For the second item, he spoke separately to two people about federal draft proposals to improve long-term care homes. The third item featured the inventor of an internet search engine for eighteenth- and nineteenth-century books. The fourth and final item was titled "the convoy approaching Ottawa." Rather than speak to a trucker, Galloway interviewed Justin Ling, a self-described "freelance investigative journalist" from Montreal, who would become the CBC's go-to reporter on the Freedom Convoy, or what the network referred to as "the so-called Freedom Convoy" or, in this case, "the convoy approaching Ottawa."

"This protest did not begin as a protest of vaccine mandates for truckers," Ling said categorically, beginning an analysis that was to give CBC Radio listeners close to the most distorted picture of the convoy possible. "It's not about the truckers, it's so much more," he said.

The convoy, Ling explained, was the brainchild of James Bauder, who held a "list of some kooky conspiracy beliefs," and who founded Canada Unity, "the organizer for the convoy." Bauder's core organizing purpose revolved around a "Memorandum of Understanding," which sought to govern the country without the prime minister or House of Commons. Bauder's group would form a committee with the Senate and the Governor General and abolish all COVID-19 vaccination requirements. Bauder had latched on to the vaccine issue, Ling said, to make his cause more topical. The convoy is not anti-mandates, it is anti-vaccines, he said. Bauder viewed all vaccines — not just COVID-19 ones — as "poison."

"There has been a sort of coalescing of a ton of anti-vaccine and far-right figures into this movement," Ling also said. As an example, he cited Pat King, "a notorious figure amongst the Canadian far right" and "one of the chief Alberta organizers for this convoy." Ling then contradicted himself. The movement did not, in fact, include "a ton" of anti-vaccine and far-right figures.

Convoy organizers "wildly inflate their numbers," he said. There might be hundreds of trucks coming to Ottawa but not thousands.

Host Galloway, after hearing of all the kooks and right-wingers, asked the natural follow-up question: "What do you think is likely to happen when this protest arrives in Ottawa this weekend?"

"I think you have to prepare for the worst," Ling said. "I don't think violence will happen Saturday, but I think it's a possibility, and I think we should be extremely concerned."

As It Happens, CBC Radio's evening newsmagazine, at least led with the convoy story but handled it just as falsely.

"The convoy is ostensibly protesting COVID-19 rules, especially the vaccine mandate for cross-border truckers," Chris Howden said to introduce the item. "But the movement has also attracted anti-vaxxers, conspiracy theorists, and right-wing extremists." He gave no examples, cited no names, and quoted no statements. Co-host Carol Off then interviewed Mike Millian, president of the Private Motor Truck Council of Canada, an association of private fleet operators.

"Mike, according to police estimates," she began, citing no specific source, "there are hundreds of vehicles that are part of this convoy but only about 100 trucks. How do you feel about these 100 truckers claiming to represent the views of thousands of truckers across the country?"

Millian replied evenly, saying he expected more than 100 trucks, he believed in peaceful protest, and he opposed the vaccine mandate for cross-border truckers.

"Do you think that the truckers are aware, though, that they're being used," Off said, pushing her point, "that this whole thing was started by, it seems, by those who believe that COVID-19 is an international conspiracy?"

Again, she quoted nobody and offered no specifics. She did, however, suggest where she was getting her questions. "It seems there's been some pretty good journalism on this," she said. "People like Justin Ling."

On CBCNN, the CBC's cable television news network, Nil Köksal floated an outright conspiracy theory of her own. Russia had been moving troops and equipment to its border with Ukraine. An invasion looked imminent. Köksal, as host of *Power & Politics*, asked Public Safety Minister Marco Mendicino if the Russians were also behind the Freedom Convoy protest. "Given Canada's support of Ukraine in this current crisis with Russia," she said, "there is concern that Russian actors could be continuing to fuel things as this protest grows but perhaps even instigating it from the outset."

Mendicino, maintaining a neutral expression, said he would let police answer that question. One week later, the CBC attached a "clarification" — not a "retraction" or a "correction" — to the online version of its story and video. "At 4:15," the note said, "there is a question about the possibility Russian actors could be fuelling or instigating a truck convoy protest headed to Parliament Hill. The question should have referenced experts' concerns that during the current tension over Ukraine, Moscow could use its cyber and disinformation capabilities to 'sow confusion' among Ukraine's allies during a crisis." Who the concerned experts were the CBC did not say.

By the eve of the official arrival in Ottawa, two Freedom Convoys had materialized. One was the Freedom Convoy as seen from behind the wheel of a long-haul rig on the highway, or from a bridge, or from the side of the road, or from a crowd at a truck stop — a celebratory coming together of common-sense, working Canadians to assert their individual liberties and collective freedoms. The other was the "so-called Freedom Convoy" fashioned by the CBC and most of the other Canadian corporate news media, a convoy of kooks, yokels, yahoos, conspiracy theorists, and right-ringers, who were possibly manipulated by a foreign, enemy government and who carried with them the potential for violence. In the coming days, the corporate media would only magnify their original portrayal, denying their listeners and readers the true picture. Elsewhere, however, word of the genuine Freedom Convoy was spreading.

"Canadian truckers rule," Elon Musk, posted to Twitter two days before the official arrival. As the world's richest man, the head of Tesla and SpaceX, with 103 million Twitter followers, he ignited a wave of international interest. The Canadian Freedom Convoy was becoming a global story.

Chapter 6

Everybody Lives by a Core Value

On Tuesday, four days before the official arrival, I delivered a mixed load to western New York State. It was a solo run, without my brother. I made a stop in Buffalo, then dropped off two skids to a hospital in Elmira, near the Pennsylvania border. For the return trip, I was to pick up bottles across town from Anchor Glass for delivery to Delta Breweries north of Toronto, but the load wasn't ready. I went online to check developments. A Canadian Press story in the *Toronto Star* caught my eye. It looked like fake news.

"GoFundMe has frozen access to the more than $4.7 million in funds raised by the trucker convoy now wending its way across the country toward Ottawa," it said.

I know people who've done GoFundMe campaigns. Every new account, especially if it's the seventh or eighth fastest-growing GoFundMe account in history, which ours was, comes under scrutiny. Who's involved? What country are they in? Is their documentation complete? Every campaign must comply with banking and international money-laundering laws, and the more successful the drive, the more careful GoFundMe has to be. The process takes time. When I checked our webpage, the progress bar still showed donations mounting minute by minute. I called Tamara.

"I've got a stupid question."

"What?"

"Is access to GoFundMe frozen?"

"I just got off the phone with their lawyers," she said, laughing. "They've been great. They said, 'Everything's fine, just give us a bit more time and we'll release everything.'"

I think of myself as a serial entrepreneur. I like to move from venture to venture as a way to develop new skills and stay engaged. Once, I patented a protective motorcycle seat pad for racers and had it manufactured and sold in the United States. Before that, I earned a gemology certificate from HRD Antwerp, Europe's leading diamond authority, when they had an office in Toronto. For two years I graded diamonds. For a time, I ran a graphics store on the campus of what until recently was called Ryerson University, renamed out of political correctness to Toronto Metropolitan University. I've lived in Medellin, Columbia, and in Miami, Florida. In 2015 I ran for Parliament. At the last minute, I replaced the nominated Conservative Party candidate in Toronto-Danforth because of a scandal. The Liberal won under Justin Trudeau's banner, but I increased the Tory vote to 10 percent from 4 percent. Now, when people ask what I do, I say I produce podcasts. I run my own online media company, with a stable of podcasts that I produce and edit. Recently, I merged the business with an online newspaper, *The National Telegraph*, or TNT.

A couple of years ago I bought a long-haul truck. My brother drove a rig part-time and wanted to upgrade. He said why not buy his truck, operate it as a side business, and we could drive in tandem together on deliveries to the United States? Hauling freight became my escape from the lockdowns. When I wasn't editing a podcast or busy with other projects, I would pick up a load at the yard and drive across the border, usually to Connecticut, or Boston, or maybe Philadelphia. Often, my brother and I would go together. We both had CB radios. We never lost touch with each other. We would sometimes end up in Connecticut at around eight-thirty or nine in the evening, go for dinner at a restaurant we like there, and hang out afterward in the back of his truck. Then I would go back to my own cab. I would boot up the OmniFocus management software on my laptop, update my to-do lists, make my schedules, write messages, and check the news, then get up the next morning and drive back.

Everybody lives by a core value. For some people it's adaptability. For others it's balance, or acceptance, or spirituality. For me it's freedom. I like the American attitude — "I'm in control of the government, the government isn't in control of me." In Canada we're subservient. We believe we serve the government, not the other way around, which is a dangerous attitude. Crossing the border during the pandemic always felt liberating. Even in states with the harshest U.S. lockdowns, such as New York, the restrictions were nothing compared to Ontario and Quebec, because almost nobody took them as earnestly as Canadians did. Only once did an American border agent ask me to put on a mask, and in Canada everybody was always masked up. Crossing between Canada and the United States during the pandemic was like crossing between East and West Berlin during the Cold War.

After talking to Tamara, I called one of the Ottawa organizers for an update.

"How many trucks are coming?"

"We're so swamped I have no idea," he said. "We keep registering people into the database. We were estimating 36,000 trucks but we could get 50,000."

"Come on, seriously."

"It's crazy. Some are coming from the United States. If everybody comes who says they're coming, plus their families, plus supporters, we could get half a million people."

I posted some of the numbers, and Jordon Peterson, bestselling author of *12 Rules for Life*, retweeted some of them. "The convoy coming out of British Columbia heading to Ottawa is now 70 kilometers long," he wrote. "American truckers are joining." His post got 44,000 likes and 7,000 retweets.

Joe Rogan also saw some of the numbers. He hosts *The Joe Rogan Experience* in Los Angeles, one of the world's most popular podcasts, said to receive eleven million views per episode. He played a clip of trucks rolling through the darkness on their way to Calgary, an endless flow of headlights on the highway.

"Do you know about this?" he asked his guest, Valentine Thomas, a sustainable-seafood advocate originally from Montreal. "Your country is in revolt. Look at this video. It's a giant convoy of trucks. That's apparently some insane amount of people, like 50,000 trucks, that are headed to Ottawa to protest the vaccine mandates by Trudeau. Because, apparently, they're all being mandated that they have to get vaccinated and they're like, 'Hey, we don't even contact anybody. We're in our truck. We just drive.'"

At another stop through New York, I heard from Tamara again. She sent me links to videos of Pat King, the first I'd heard of him. He was speaking into the camera on TikTok.

"The only way that — and I'm going to say it out loud — the only way that this is going to be solved is bullets," he said in a clip posted the previous month. "And yeah I said it. That's the only way something's going to happen. A massive revolution on a huge scale."

"Trudeau, someone's going to make you catch a bullet one day," he said in another snippet. "To the rest of this government — someone's going to fuckin do yas in. You sons of bitches."

In a third, he warned that the white European population would be replaced by non-European immigrants. "It's called depopulation of the Caucasian race, or the Anglo-Saxon," he said. "And that's what the goal is, to depopulate the Anglo-Saxon race, because they are the ones with the strongest bloodlines."

"I'm not a nice person," he said in a fourth.

"Tamara, who is this clown?" I said. "He's going on about the white race? What is this?"

"Oh, he's a nightmare. I'm trying to get him off the convoy."

"Send him home now."

He won't go. Can you put together a statement that Pat King is not an organizer of the convoy?"

"Gladly."

We were using the GoFundMe page as a community bulletin board and for issuing press releases. I included James Bauder in the statement. "Patrick King only represents himself and does not represent any of us who started Freedom Convoy 2022/Freedom Convoy Canada," I wrote in part. "Canada Unity, led by James Bauder, is also an external group that tagged along with our convoy…. Canada Unity has its own GoFundMe and mission statement completely separate from Freedom Convoy 2022/Freedom Convoy Canada.

"We have encouraged these groups and all other groups in support of Freedom Convoy 2022/Freedom Convoy Canada to remain peaceful and moderate in their tone and rhetoric," the release continued. "We want everyone to be safe and to remember this experience… as one of the most positive experiences of their lives."

It was the best we could do. We were the Freedom Convoy. We couldn't order anybody to go home. We knew King could get us into trouble, but sometimes freedom is a messy business.

Chapter 7

Please Remain Calm and Loving

I dropped off the bottles north of Toronto and drove home to get ready for Ottawa. On Thursday morning, Tamara and I talked by phone for three hours. She was crossing Ontario with BigRed, and I would be leaving the next day. I had about twenty other things to do, and interview requests were coming in, including one from *Tucker Carlson Tonight*, which was getting 3.41 million viewers a night on Fox News. The producer asked if I could get to a studio on Don Mills Road, not far from me, and we would go live from there. I didn't have time to get nervous.

"Tell me why you're doing this," Carlson said after introducing me. "What's the point of this convoy?"

"Simple," I said. "We want two things. We want to get rid of the vaccine mandates and the passports. The passports — that's the really concerning one."

I told him about returning to Canada through Buffalo the day before. I had the ArriveCAN app downloaded to an old phone that I wasn't using for anything else. It had no SIM card and no phone number, but it was connected to U.S. WiFi.

"Yesterday was my first time ever crossing the border in my truck with my digital passport," I said. "I held my phone up to the border agent to give him the QR code. You know what he said to me? 'Oh, it's okay, I don't need it.'

"I said, 'What do you mean you don't need it?'

"He said, 'Your phone already popped up on my screen and it's correlated to your passport.'

"Think of that," I told Carlson. "Can you believe that? They know everybody who's coming up to the border before they're there, and they're tracking them. Maybe it's outlandish [to say] but what's to prevent the government from introducing that across Canada and not limiting it to just the border…? Are they going to be trading intelligence back and forth between Canada and the U.S., tracking cellphones? We have no idea, but this is where it is going if this does not stop. That's why this is the line. This is where it ends."

As I headed to my car afterward, I started going over the interview in my head. I should have looked at the camera more. At first, I wasn't sure where it was, and I was looking at it sideways. I should have smiled more, too. Right across the country, the convoy was generating euphoria, and I wanted to put that across. As I was going through my self-critique, I started getting messages. Carlson's producer had uploaded the segment to Twitter, and people were congratulating me, one after another. Finally, after a few thank-yous, I put away the phone and drove home.

The next day was Friday. Time to get to Ottawa. A friend was coming with me but wouldn't arrive until after lunch, giving me a chance to do an interview with Glenn Beck, the former Fox News host now with his own network, TheBlaze. He sounded surprised to hear about a mass protest in the land of peace, order, and good government.

"In Canada, Canadians just don't do this, they just don't rise up," Beck said to introduce the piece. "They're kind of like, I don't know, 'It's cold outside. Do we have to march in protest?' I grew up on the border of Canada, and they're very calm and peaceful people and everything else, and they don't get riled up real easily. Well, they're riled up, and there's a truck convoy now to Ottawa, it's a Freedom Convoy.... This is massive, massive.... What are you protesting, specifically?"

"There are two general areas that we are most concerned with," I said. "One is the authoritarian mandates — the lack of freedom of choice — and the other is this app."

I told him about the Canadian border agent picking up my data without me having to show the QR code. The ArriveCAN app — I was still upset. You never knew when it was transmitting, who it was transmitting to, or what information it was sending. I also told him about the crowds cheering from bridges right across the country, and holding up signs saying "We Love You" and "Freedom." In Canada, no political party — federal or provincial — opposes the vaccine mandates or objects to the QR-code vaccine passport, I said. Rival political parties no longer exist, and the corporate media are lost in groupthink.

"We have a Uni-party," I said. "The truckers have become the Official Opposition, and this is the outlet that people are using to speak. That's why there's almost $7 million in donations there in a week. It's not about the money. They don't have a place to park their vote because they don't have a voice in our system anymore."

Beck warmed to the theme. He had just published a book called *The Great Reset*, taking the name that the World Economic Forum in Davos, Switzerland, had given to their socialist vision of a post-COVID-19 world. He played a clip of a woman speaking at Davos about how unelected global elites can "come together and design and do beautiful things" for the world.

"Listen to them," Beck said. "'We can gather together and we can make decisions.' They're cutting us out of all of these decisions... the arrogance."

He finished by giving me a rousing send-off.

"What you're doing, BJ, is incredibly important," he said, "and hopefully it will inspire millions more all around the world to stand up, because we are truly on the verge of losing our rights that make us human."

I was almost ready for Ottawa. I was feeling the butterflies. More than ever, I wanted everything to go as smoothly and as flawlessly as possible, and on the GoFundMe page I posted a special appeal to the truckers and their supporters. I wanted to reinforce the positive energy of the cheering crowds. Outsiders can be expected to try to sabotage our movement, I wrote. Be on the lookout for aggressive behaviour. "Please remain calm and loving toward one another."

I laid out a few ground rules:

• Do not enter any government building under any circumstances. Critics will draw a comparison to demonstrators who entered the U.S. Capitol Building on January 6, 2021.

• Treat all police officers with respect, even if they issue you a citation.

• If you see individuals attempting to bait truckers and attendees into conflict, report them to the police and our staff.
• Do not make any type of threat. Threats lead to escalation, which can lead to violence.
• Do your best to stifle any aggressive rhetoric.

"If we keep calm and show love, good things could happen," I wrote. "The government could reverse its policy on COVID-19 passports and vaccine mandates, as the UK government just did. Even if the Canadian government digs in, however, we will meet new friends, develop relationships, maybe fall in love. This could be the first step in a long journey to a new golden age of freedom and understanding."

As trucks streamed into the nation's capital that day, police helped direct them downtown, a courtesy they would later regret. Some drivers turned directly onto Wellington Street, the thoroughfare running past the Parliament Buildings and the Prime Minister's Office opposite. The street is four lanes wide. Police instructed the truckers to double-park in the two northernmost lanes, leaving two lanes open to traffic. Sometime before Saturday morning, a third lane would also fill up, leaving one lane free for police and emergency vehicles. At a choice spot opposite the Peace Tower and the eternal flame, drivers would soon make way for a boom truck, a long, flatbed truck of the type typically used for delivering construction materials. A hydraulic boom hoists supplies on and off. The owner positioned the boom straight into the air to fly an oversized Canadian flag. He also positioned loudspeakers on the flatbed and electrical generators underneath, literally setting the stage for the demonstration.

We were about to engage in the most massive act of civil disobedience the country had ever seen. Long-haul trucks would dominate the downtown streets. Truckers would sound their air horns. We would exercise our right to protest the coercive, unjust mandates, and we would keep our resistance non-violent. In the spirit of Mahatma Gandhi's philosophy of *satyagraha*, we would seek not victory for ourselves and defeat for our adversaries. We would seek a new harmony. Viewed pragmatically, our success depended almost entirely on the government's openness to listen. Prime Minister Trudeau might choose to engage with us, or he might not.

Chapter 8

The Heart of the Protest

On Saturday morning, Day One, we headed downtown. We were staying in the suburbs with Tom Quiggin, host of *The Quiggin Report* podcast, which he and I were doing at the time. He is also an ex-military intelligence officer who was helping to establish an "operations centre," a hub from which to coordinate the demonstration from a logistics and public-safety perspective. The three of us rode the LRT to the Rideau Centre shopping complex and walked up the hill to the Swiss Hotel, a three-storey, limestone building from 1872, slightly removed from the main protest area.

The front vestibule led downstairs to a low-slung reception lobby jammed with people. Along one wall lay a counter teeming with platters of scrambled eggs, bacon, bagels, hot dogs, and sandwiches, and a big coffee urn. Along the opposite wall people had piled their backpacks and parkas, and sometimes sweaters and hoodies. The room was warm with bodies, all milling around exchanging information and rumours.

I spotted Tamara. Her back was to me but I recognized her instantly — five-foot nothing, long brown hair, black puffer jacket, sunglasses pushed to the top of her head. When I made my way over and gave her a little poke, she spun around and jumped at me like a puppy dog. She got quite emotional.

"Oh my God," she said giving me a big hug, tears welling in her eyes. "I can't believe it. This is so amazing."

Everybody was trying to cope with the enormity of what we started. Road captains had guided thousands of trucks to Ottawa, cheered by hundreds of thousands of people along the way, turning a small, protest idea into a national phenomenon. Now we faced staggering challenges. People were dropping off food donations, sometimes by the crateful, sometimes in even larger quantities. People were offering diesel fuel by the tankful, and jerry cans of fuel by the pickup-truck load. Obtaining food and fuel was not the concern. Getting the supplies to the trucks was. We needed a distribution system, an organization to allocate the provisions and a fleet of drivers to deliver them. We needed to keep the protest running.

In a conference room off the lobby, volunteer coordinators were working out a basic infrastructure. The hotel is built on a slope, so that light flooded through windows along the back wall. A fireplace filled one corner. An upright piano stood by the door. The main action was taking place at a great, wooden, square table at the centre of the room, jammed elbow-to-elbow with people at phones and laptops, all working at different tasks. No single person appeared to be in charge. Volunteers for a local group called "Adopt a Trucker" were setting up a billeting service for visitors needing a place to stay. Others were creating a shuttle service for drivers who needed to go somewhere in town without having to move their rig. Still others were working out a system to allow an outlying truck to take the parking spot of a downtown truck that had to leave for a job.

Former RCMP Corporal Daniel Bulford, once a sniper assigned to the prime minister's protection detail, until he lost his job for declining the vaccine, took charge of a security committee. He established a type of neighbourhood watch system and a structure for reporting any act of vandalism or unwanted activity that might bring the protest into disrepute. To keep lanes open to emergency services traffic and to coordinate safety issues, Bulford also opened avenues of communication with City Hall, the RCMP, the OPP, the Ottawa Police Service, and the Parliamentary Protective Service.

"I've been part of many big events in Ottawa," Bulford said later, "and when I came here I thought, 'What have I gotten myself into? This is a massive task, there's very little time, but we don't have a choice. We've got to make this work.'"

Nobody will ever know how many trucks joined the Freedom Convoy, or tried to join. Nobody counted the trucks slow-rolling in various parts of the country. In Ottawa, Brigitte Belton's group was directed to the Canadian War Museum, and, when the lot filled up, the hundreds of trucks behind her on the Sir John A. Macdonald Parkway simply parked where they were, tip to tail, filling the right lane for kilometres. Three lanes of Wellington Street filled up, along with the parking lanes on neighbouring streets. Some drivers claimed spots at Confederation Park opposite City Hall off Elgin Street. Hundreds more followed police instructions to park at the Ottawa baseball stadium's massive lot, slightly removed from downtown on Coventry Road. The outpost quickly turned into a food-distribution base and fuel depot, dotted with supply tents, latrines, and eventually saunas and hot tubs. Other clusters formed elsewhere in the city. Still others holed up in nearby towns and villages and in farmers' fields. Many drivers, having no way to enter the city and perhaps feeling they had made their point, turned around and headed home.

At three o'clock, the three of us left the Swiss and headed on foot to the heart of the protest. The sky was bright and sunny, the temperature minus twenty degrees Celsius. The wind-chill factor put it at minus thirty. People usually hate going out in such cold. We followed Rideau Street to the Château Laurier Hotel, one of the country's grand, old railway hotels, an architectural jewel, and, in the distance, we could see crowds surging toward us over the Alexandra Bridge from Quebec, like a mass migration. The police had barricaded the bridge to stop more trucks from crossing, and people were leaving their vehicles to walk.

"Hey, let's check this out," I said.

Manoeuvring against the flow, we tried to get close to the bridge. From as far as the eye could see, thousands of people advanced toward us, some waving flags — the Canadian Maple Leaf and Quebec Fleurdelisé. Others carried signs saying "freedom" or "liberté." Eventually, we turned around and moved with the packed crowd. With the Houses of Parliament and National Library visible on the cliff to our right, we followed the walkways through Major's Hill Park, slowed at a narrow passage between the Château Laurier and the Rideau Canal, and squeezed through the pedestrian gates onto Wellington Street, everybody cheering like wanderers arrived in a promised land. For two years, Quebec had been under some of the harshest lockdowns in the country and the world. A nighttime curfew had been recently lifted, but Premier Francois Legault had newly imposed a vaccine requirement on anybody wanting to enter a Walmart, a Costco, a

Home Depot, or a liquor store and was proposing a new tax — a "health contribution," he called it — on anybody declining the vaccines.

On Wellington Street opposite Parliament, everybody was laughing and joking and hugging each other. Police officially estimated the crowd at 15,000 to 18,000 people. The number might have been higher. Nobody had ever seen anything like it. Every July 1, Ottawa throws a lavish Canada Day celebration with dancers and rock bands, but this was more spontaneous, more boisterous, more outrageous. There was no script and no program. Truckers honked their horns, filling the air with discordant sound. An indigenous drum circle thumped rhythmically. Stereo systems blasted country-and-western music and French-Canadian folk tunes. People were handing out free earplugs.

"My parents woke me up for the moon landing, and I brought my kids to see this," one man said. Another hoisted his son to an open cab window saying, "My boy wants to meet a trucker," and the driver reached for the boy and showed him how to pull the cord to sound the horn. Some people handed cash to the truckers. One man passed a $100 bill through a window, and the driver folded it into his breast pocket as casually as if he had been accepting donations all day. Two days earlier, GoFundMe had released $1 million to a TD Bank account as a first payment to the truckers, but the bank refused to forward the money. The street swarmed with a cross-section of people not normally seen at a demonstration. Soccer moms in pricey goose-down jackets mingled with tradesmen in scuffed work boots and wool caps. Quebecers from across the river mixed with visitors from Alberta and Saskatchewan, as though the Quebec Winter Carnival had spilled into the Calgary Stampede. Some people carried signs saying "Truck You Trudeau" — impossible to translate. Others just yelled "Fuck Trudeau" and "Yeah, fuck Trudeau," often in a French accent.

Giant semis dominated the streetscape. People were used to seeing long-haul rigs on the highway but not parked up close, at the city centre, en masse. With their engines idling in the cold, chugging softly, exhaling vapour, the bright winter sun glinting off their fenders, the machines looked powerful and inspiring. They looked as solid and enduring as the Parliament Buildings themselves. For the first time in my life, I felt a rush of national pride and togetherness. That afternoon, I gave an interview to a Quebec journalist writing for a publication in France. "This is incredible," she said. "I used to be a separatist, and today I bought my first Canadian flag."

Chapter 9

The Small Fringe Minority

The target of the protest, Prime Minister Justin Trudeau, left town just as the trucks were arriving. His reason kept changing. First, he said he had been in close proximity to somebody who tested positive for COVID-19. He tested negative himself, he said, but had to self-isolate for five days. Then he said he and his family had to relocate for "security reasons." He was concerned about potential violence. A couple of days later, in a video news conference from what was called "an undisclosed location," he returned to his first explanation. Two of his children had tested positive for COVID-19 and that morning so had he. "I'm feeling fine," he posted to Twitter, "and I'll continue to work remotely this week while following public health guidelines. Everyone, please get vaccinated and get boosted."

Perhaps more than any other event since he was first elected prime minister in 2015, the Freedom Convoy brought out

Trudeau's true character. His response to the mass demonstration in Ottawa, and to sister rallies that continued in towns and cities from coast to coast, was to reveal his cowardice, his petulance, his hypocrisy, his contempt for popular feeling, his inability to generate conciliation or compromise, and, ultimately, his attraction to authoritarian power.

His cowardice surfaced with his speedy departure, but his petulance also quickly emerged. Earlier, Trudeau had characterized unvaccinated people generally as "often misogynists, also often racists," and had asked, "Do we tolerate these people?" Three days before the convoy's scheduled arrival in the city, at a formal news conference, he again irritably dismissed the truckers.

"The small, fringe minority of people who are on their way to Ottawa, who are holding unacceptable views, that they are expressing, do not represent the views of Canadians who have been there for each other," he said. The convoy participants, he also told a Canadian Press reporter two days later, are "a very troubling, small, but very vocal minority of Canadians who are lashing out at science, at government, at society, at mandates, and public health advice."

Misogynists, racists, fringe minority, people with unacceptable views lashing out at society — the slurs evoked Hillary Clinton's insults against Donald Trump supporters during the 2016 U.S. presidential campaign. "You could put half of Trump's supporters into what I call the basket of deplorables — right?" she said. "The racist, sexist, homophobic, xenophobic, Islamophobic — you name it."

Clinton backpedaled the next day, calling her comments "grossly generalistic," and she never repeated them. Trudeau, on the other hand, never recanted. Far from it. He would repeat the slurs many times, and it was hard not to notice that they might apply more to himself than to anybody at the Freedom Convoy.

"Misogynist" technically refers to somebody who hates women, but Trudeau often uses the word to mean "sexist," somebody who disrespects or discriminates against women. After the 2015 election, as though to showcase his own enlightened views, he filled half his cabinet positions with women. Later, however, he expelled his two most senior female ministers — Justice Minister Jodi Wilson-Raybould and Health Minister Jane Philpot — when they took a principled stand against him in the 2019 SNC-Lavalin scandal.

A simpler example of Trudeau's treatment of women might be his alleged groping. In 2000, when he was twenty-eight years old, he attended a music festival to support avalanche safety in the town of Creston, B.C. Afterward, in an unsigned newspaper column, a female reporter complained of him "groping" and "inappropriately handling" her at the event. "I'm sorry," the woman quoted Trudeau as saying at the time. "If I had known you were reporting for a national paper, I never would have been so forward." When wider awareness of the encounter surfaced in 2018, when Trudeau was prime minister, the woman said she considered the matter closed. Trudeau did not directly deny the original claim.

"I don't remember any negative interactions that day at all," he told an initial news scrum. A few days later, he pivoted to make the issue not about him but about "we."

"I'm responsible for my side of the interaction which certainly, as I said, I don't feel was in any way untoward," he told reporters outside the House of Commons. "But at the same time this lesson that we are learning, and I'll be blunt about it, often a man experiences an interaction as being benign, or not inappropriate, and a woman, particularly in a professional context, can experience it differently, and we have to respect that and reflect on it."

Trudeau's "racist" charge carried a particular irony. In 2019, three photos and a video surfaced of him wearing the kind of theatrical blackface makeup once used to racially stereotype black people. One photo dating from his high school years showed him wearing an Afro wig and blackface onstage singing "Day-O (The Banana Boat Song)," about Jamaican night workers loading bananas onto ships. Two other still photos dated to his time as a high-school teacher, at the age of twenty-nine. They showed him at an "Arabian Nights" party costumed as Aladdin, wearing a turban and either blackface or brownface — the picture is in black-and-white — over his face, neck, and hands. The lone video dated to his time as a summer-camp counsellor when he was in his early twenties. The footage shows him wearing black makeup over his face, neck, arms, hands, and legs, and he appears to have stuck a banana-shaped object down the front of his pants. No audio is attached, but at one point he raises his arms monkey-like and opens and closes his mouth.

"Darkening your face, regardless of the context or the circumstances, is always unacceptable because of the racist history of blackface," Trudeau said when the material surfaced publicly during the 2019 election campaign. "I should have understood that then, and I never should have done it." Asked if more examples of him in blackface might yet surface, he suggested he could well have worn it on other occasions. "I am wary of being definitive about this because the recent pictures that came out I had not remembered," he said.

One thing is for sure. Of the 15,000 to 18,000 or more people who took part in the Freedom Convoy protest on opening day, not one was known to have exhibited behaviour as racist as that of the prime minister as a teenager and young adult.

"Fringe minority" means both small and disreputable. Trudeau's Liberals might not have been fringe but unequivocally they constituted a minority. When the convoys arrived, the prime minister was leading his second minority government in a row. In the 2021 election, he won with 32 percent of the votes cast, the lowest of a wining party in a hundred years. The Conservatives received more votes than the Liberals — 34 percent — but took fewer seats. "It would appear that the so-called 'fringe minority' is actually the government," Elon Musk quipped on Twitter. People at the demonstration on Saturday, to mock Trudeau, waved placards saying "Proud Member of the Fringe Minority" and "We the Fringe," a play on the Toronto Raptors' rallying cry "We the North."

With his insults, Trudeau showed himself as petulant and hypocritical, but his hypocrisy extended further. He had long made a show of supporting peaceful political protest. Instead of hiding, he occasionally joined in. Two years earlier, he had endorsed a "No Justice No Peace" demonstration, often referred to as a Black Lives Matter protest, over an American issue. It concerned the death of George Floyd, the black man in Minneapolis who died while pinned to the ground, knee to the neck, by a white police officer, Derek Chauvin. Trudeau and others also dropped to one knee, not to mimic the officer but in solidarity with American athletes who refused to stand for the American national anthem as a protest against anti-black racism.

Later the same year, Trudeau went out of his way to support a protest in India. Farmers mainly from Punjab and Haryana provinces were demonstrating — at that stage peacefully — against new agricultural laws passed by the Indian Parliament, and police were attacking them with batons, tear gas, and water cannons. Trudeau sided with the farmers against the Indian government. "Canada will always be there to defend the right of peaceful protest," he said in a video address to a Canadian Sikh congress. "We believe in the importance of dialogue."

When the Indian government said the remarks "constitute an unacceptable interference in our internal affairs" and, if continued, "would have a seriously damaging impact on ties between India and Canada," Trudeau doubled down. "Canada will always stand up for the right of peaceful protest anywhere around the world," he said. His words were to come back to haunt him.

Chapter 10

The Virus is the Media

Saturday's opening festivities continued long into the night. Truckers continued their honking cacophony, and after midnight people set off fireworks, lighting the sky over Parliament not so much in protest as in national celebration. Togetherness and friendship prevailed. The police issued no parking tickets, towed away no vehicles, made no arrests, and reported no violence. Our most optimistic expectations were realized.

Across the world, people took notice. In Canberra, Australia, organizers announced a matching "Millions March Against Mandatory Vaccination." Dozens of other protests involving campers, trucks of various sizes, and Canadian flags were being organized in Paris, Brussels, Vienna, the New Zealand capital of Wellington, and in Israel on the highway from Tel Aviv to Jerusalem. On Saturday night in Conroe, Texas, former U.S. President Donald Trump paid tribute. "We want those great

Canadian truckers to know that we're with them all the way," he told a massive crowd. "They're doing more to defend American freedom than our own leaders, by far."

Opening day could not have gone better, but the Canadian corporate news media presented an alternate demonstration, like their alternate convoy. They reported opening day as a series of six scandals — six instances of shocking, disreputable behaviour.

Two were said to have taken place at the National War Memorial. It stands at the centre of a traffic island where Wellington and Elgin Streets meet, across from the Château Laurier Hotel. Bronze sculptures depict a troop of First World War soldiers passing through a granite arch, overseen by the allegorical figures of Freedom and Peace. At the south end of the monument, cordoned off in the summertime and watched by ceremonial guards, three small steps lead to the Tomb of the Unknown Soldier. On the day of the protest, there was no cordon and no guard, and the tomb was mostly covered in snow and ice. At one point, an exuberant woman ran up the steps, wound her arm in the air, whooped and hooted, shouted "freedom," pumped her legs for emphasis, bending her knees, and after a total of several seconds ran back down. Phone video captured the moment for Twitter, and news outlets reported that protesters — plural — were "dancing on the grave of the unknown soldier." Defence Minister Anita Anand called the behaviour "beyond reprehensible." The chief of the Canadian defence staff, General Wayne Eyre, labelled the act one of desecration. "I am sickened to see protesters dance on the Tomb of the Unknown Soldier and desecrate the National War Memorial," he said. "Those involved should hang their heads in shame."

Three months later, Ottawa police tracked down the alleged offender. She had had no idea she was standing on a grave and had meant no disrespect. No charges were laid. "A woman who resides out of province was identified," the police said in a news release. "She was spoken to, showed remorse for her actions, and police are confident she will not re-offend."

Also at the war memorial, yellow stains were noticed in the snow the next morning at a semi-secluded spot next to the arch. Nobody seemed to have witnessed the cause, but the stains were assumed to be of human origin — "protesters urinating on the site," Global News said. However inexcusable, public urination and even vomiting are also known to happen at the same spot on Canada Day, when revellers party into the night. Politicians don't usually comment on such cases, but this time they did, beginning with Veterans Affairs Minister Lawrence MacAulay. "Completely unacceptable," he said, "[a] flagrant desecration and disrespect of our sacred monuments." Conservative Leader Erin O'Toole, a former veterans affairs minister, added his condemnation. "I support the right to peacefully protest but that should not be confused with blatant disrespect for the men and women who have served, inspired, and protected our country," he said. "The individuals in question should be "ashamed."

A third alleged wrongdoing involved the Terry Fox statue on Wellington Street, directly opposite Parliament's Centre Block. Fox ranks as one of the country's most beloved heroes. As a young man, he lost his right leg to cancer and, in a campaign to raise money for cancer research, ran 5,373 kilometres (3,340 miles) from the eastern shore of Newfoundland nearly to Thunder Bay, on Lake Superior. When his cancer returned, he had to quit. He died less than a year later in 1981 at the age of twenty-two.

The statue is mounted on a low plinth, between a heavily travelled sidewalk and an open plaza. It is readily accessible, with the Instagram selfie in mind. On Day One, freedom demonstrators swarmed the area, and some of them adopted the statue as a kind of mascot. They fitted it with a "Mandate Freedom" sign and a hockey cap displaying a Maple Leaf. Somebody also draped a Canadian flag over Fox's shoulders in the way many people in the crowd were wearing it. The CBC, CTV, and other outlets called the actions a "defacement," as though demonstrators had treated the statue the same way activists across the country for months had attacked, thrown paint at, and destroyed statues of Queen Victoria, Egerton Ryerson, and Canada's first prime minister, Sir John A. MacDonald. Following the media outcry over the Fox statue, demonstrators respectfully removed their paraphernalia.

The fourth and fifth supposed transgressions were said to involve Confederate and Nazi flags. The Confederate flag, or Southern Cross, was the battle flag of the southern United States during the American Civil War, in which the Confederacy resisted the abolition of slavery. The flag is commonly viewed now as a racist symbol, and on Saturday morning a solitary man carried one on a pole over his shoulder, directly opposite the Peace Tower. He flourished a high-quality custom-made version, with a tractor-trailer superimposed on it. The man was disguised. He wore a black balaclava over his head, with openings only for the mouth and eyes and the eye holes covered by sunglasses.

Initially, the flag-bearer tried to walk past Maxime Bernier, leader of the populist People's Party of Canada, as though to implicate Bernier in racism. Political handlers chased the intruder away, but a moment later three professional photographers snapped high-quality photos of the flag among the protestors. Reporter Alexa Lavoie, for the independent Rebel News outlet, later identified the photographers. All had Liberal Party connections. One had been Liberal Prime Minister Paul Martin's official photographer. That day he sold his pictures to Getty

Images. Another sold his photos to iPolitics, owned by the *Toronto Star*. The third sold his to other legacy media outlets. All shot their photos from almost the same spot at the same instant, suggesting a setup. None responded to Lavoie's requests for comment. Seconds after the shots were taken, the flag-bearer disappeared into the crowd and the flag was never seen again, except in newspapers and on television.

Four pictures taken of a Nazi flag on Saturday caused a particular sensation. One was taken in the park behind the Château Laurier. The other three were snapped a few minutes later, in quick succession, on the walkway alongside the hotel leading to Wellington Street. In her investigation, Lavoie established that the photo in the park was staged with nobody else around. As for the series of three, judging from the camera angle, she concluded that the photographer was pre-positioned at a spot cordoned off for the winter, opposite the hotel on the canal bank. No cluster of protesters was gathered on the bank and nobody just happened to snap a photo. It was a setup. The flag was never seen among the protesters, and after the photos were taken it was never seen again.

The photographer gave the shots to Justin Ling, the perfect patsy, the Montreal freelancer selling convoy stories to the CBC, the *Toronto Star*, and *Maclean's* magazine. "Someone just sent these my way," he posted to Twitter, keeping the photographer's name secret. "More photos of the Nazi flag that was spotted at today's convoy protest." A few days later, Ling also accused Conservative Party MPs of expressing support for the truckers "no matter how many photos of Nazi and Confederate flags have flown in the crowd."

The sixth alleged offense was said to have taken place at a soup kitchen for the homeless. In Lower Town, away from Parliament Hill, the director of the Shepherds of Good Hope kitchen said "staff and volunteers were verbally harassed by people who came to the kitchen looking for meals…. One of the people who used services in the shelter was assaulted." The offenders were from the Freedom Convoy, the director said. She offered no evidence. Nobody was identified. No suspect could be questioned. At the same time, all along Wellington and neighbouring streets, truckers were cooking food and giving it away to anybody who approached, including the homeless. On social media, videos showed truckers filling knapsacks for the homeless with food. "Don't ever leave," one grateful man told them.

Taken together, the six episodes made slim pickings for critics, but in the coming days and weeks corporate news outlets featured them over and over, almost to the exclusion of anything else about the demonstration. The media and Trudeau functioned like a tag-team. Reporters would publish their stories and broadcast their clips. The prime minister and his officials would denounce the protesters. The reporters would cover the denunciations, and the program hosts, commentators, guests, and newspaper editorial boards would express condemnation and moral outrage.

Chapter 11

Fooling the Censor Bots

Day Two dawned with an extreme-weather alert from Environment Canada. The overnight temperature hit minus twenty-eight degrees, close to a record low for the date. By mid-morning thermometers were registering only minus fifteen. Still, the crowds were out. By the thousands, under a sunny, blue sky, people strolled up and down Wellington Street talking to truckers, waving flags, handing out coffee, and sharing experiences. The enormous trucks, doubling as mobile homes, already looked well entrenched, like houseboats permanently docked at the marina.

At 11 a.m., Tamara and I hosted a religious service from the boom-truck stage. It was positioned perpendicular to the curb, helping to frame what became the demonstration's central square, at Wellington and Metcalfe Streets. The stage ran along the west side of the square. Along the east side, three abreast, sat a row of big, showy, classic-looking, custom-built cabs, with chrome grills and exhaust pipes. Between the two lines lay an open commons where people could gather for the service, although so many hundreds of people came that they clogged the street and sidewalks on all sides. Somebody extended the boom-crane with the Canadian flag into the air, signalling that the event was about to start.

Tamara and I introduced the presenters. In the cold, words puffed from our mouths like speech balloons in a cartoon. The horn-honking subsided. An indigenous clan mother from the Northwest Territories spoke of love, not division, and a singer led the crowd in "O Canada" and "Amazing Grace." A black, evangelical minister from Montreal, Carlos Norbal, translated everything into French.

Then the featured speaker took the platform, Henry Hildebrandt, a firebrand preacher from the Mennonite Church of God in Aylmer, Ontario, wearing rimless eye-glasses and a trim, grey beard. Instead of a winter hat, he made do with wraparound earmuffs, and instead of a bulky parka, like the ones seen everywhere in the crowd, he wore a dark, wool jacket.

"If it sounds like I'm mad, I'm just passionate, don't worry about it," he said, then pointed to Parliament Hill. "You see our Peace Tower? In the south window of our Peace Tower, I stress Peace Tower, we have these beautiful words engraved. I'll read you the words. Truckers, they're a real encouragement for you."

He was talking about the Assembly of Remembrance, a set of stained-glass windows at the front of the tower facing south, above the arched main entrance to Parliament. One of the panels bears an inscription from the ancient Athenian statesman Pericles. "Freedom is the sure possession of those alone who have the courage to defend it," Hildebrandt quoted. Cheers went up from the crowd.

"Freedom is the sure possession of those alone who have the courage to defend it," he repeated, bringing louder cheers. Forcefully, he quoted the line a third time, and the crowd roared.

After the service we held our first news conference. As convoy spokesperson, part of my job was to speak to the news media, and many of the convoy organizers thought that meant giving daily news briefings to the corporate media. To me, talking to outlets like the CBC and the *Toronto Star* was a waste of time. They weren't reporting the story honestly. Before the convoys even reached Ottawa, the *Toronto Star* ran an editorial cartoon showing a truck labelled "Disinformation and Extremism" running over a beaver, a national Canadian symbol. All corporate media — print, radio, and television — were compromised. When Trudeau was first elected, he boosted the CBC's budget by $150 million a year. Subsequently, he approved subsidies for all other corporate news outlets, totalling $600 million over five years. In 2021, three months before the last federal election, he announced an additional $20.5 million to small periodicals and weekly newspapers, a $10 million "top-up fund" to select print, radio, and television outlets, and an additional $10 million over two years for what he called a Local Journalism Initiative. All establishment news media took money from the Trudeau government. None could be trusted to report a federal political story impartially.

I had another reason for ignoring the CBC and CTV. If I were to give an interview to *The National*, CBC's flagship television news show, I might appear for twenty seconds and get 263,000 viewers, the ratings figure released for March 1, 2022. Tucker Carlson gave me eight minutes on a show that registered 3.41 million viewers. Our media strategy, I told colleagues, was not to hold news conferences for establishment Canadian media. Instead, our approach was to take our message to social-media platforms and to the global, independent news media, especially the international cable and podcast shows. I set a goal: 100 million views globally the first week. Whether I achieved it or not, I don't know. I might have exceeded it. Some analytics you can access, others you can't.

At our first news conference, Chris "BigRed" Barber, Tamara, and I spoke to independent media only. We weren't banning corporate reporters from the demonstration. It was open to everybody. No matter what their affiliation, any reporter was free to roam among the protesters and speak to whomever they pleased. I just thought, "Let's give the alternative media a chance to shine." It would be an experiment. If the corporate reporters wanted to hear what we had to say, let them listen to the independent-media livestreams.

Alexa Lavoie of Rebel News and Andrew Lawton from True North could be counted on to ask good questions. The *Post Millennial* and the *National Telegraph* online news agencies were welcome. The *Epoch Times* newspaper qualified, as did Rupa Subramanya, a freelancer who wrote for the corporate *National Post* but also for independent publications. Live-streamers Keean Bexte and Salman Sima asked to be included, and so did others. For our first session, we easily filled an upstairs room at the Swiss Hotel.

"How many people make up your core organizational team?" somebody asked.

"There are multiple layers of people helping out," Barber said, breaking down the numbers. The core group might number forty or fifty people, handling communications, liaising with police bodies, overseeing security, coordinating the trucks, compiling registrations, and supervising food, water, clothing, and fuel logistics. Beyond that, hundreds of people were involved in the volunteer Adopt-a-Trucker effort, billeting people in their homes and attending to other needs. A third layer extended into the thousands. It wasn't an organization, it was a grassroots movement. "It's organic," he said. "There are multiple layers of people helping out... The Sikh community is out in numbers at all the truck stops, handing out food, handing out blankets. That's not coming from the convoy [organization]. It's coming from the Sikh community."

Tamara spoke emotionally of people she had met at truck-stop rallies across the country, people who lost their livelihoods to the lockdowns, a man whose mother died alone in a long-term care home closed to visitors, and a mother with a twelve-year-old boy with multiple sclerosis, who was losing mobility in his hips because the swimming pool where he exercised was ordered shut. "A leader brings people together, not destroys them and tears them apart," she said.

What do you expect when Parliament resumes next week? somebody asked. A few prominent Conservative MPs had been wandering through the crowds talking to truckers, but the Conservative leader was holding back.

"You're going to see shifts in the direction of the Conservative Party," I said. "Erin O'Toole is going to be replaced as leader. Party members come up and tell me they're supportive [of the convoy] and I say, 'Great, get out there and show yourself. Pull Erin O'Toole and name an interim leader. We look forward to meeting the new leader of the Conservative Party."

Another part of my job was to feed social media. The trick was not to get censored. Major platforms routinely banned anybody questioning official COVID-19 edicts. A "Freedom Convoy" Twitter account would have been cancelled outright. To work around the bots — the web censorship robots — I used personal accounts. I used my personal Twitter account, Tamara's account, my media company account, whatever accounts I had access to, and I would frequently change up the hashtags. I used #FreedomConvoy, #FreedomConvoyCanada, #FreedomConvoy 2022, #FreedomConvoy22, #Convoy22, and #Convoy2022. To a human they all conveyed the same idea, but to a censor bot they all looked different. A bot doesn't know what "Convoy2022" or "FreedomConvoy" mean, only that they are two completely different sets of binary that have nothing to do with each other. Supporters created other hashtags I hadn't thought of — #truckerconvoy and #convoyforfreedom — and at one point we had five convoy-related hashtags all trending. Over the course of the protest, we were able to freely advocate for an end to government vaccine mandates and the QR passport. Our Twitter feeds racked up twenty or thirty million impressions.

I also follow the podcast world. *Tucker Carlson Tonight* isn't a podcast but segments often run like a podcast on YouTube, and my appearances on Tucker Carlson and Glenn Beck gave the convoy an early boost. Over the coming days, I would do other U.S. shows: *Louder with Crowder*, with Steven Crowder; *The Rubin Report* with Dave Rubin; the *Breitbart News Daily Podcast*, with Alex Marlow; and a *DailyWire* podcast with Candace Owens. I would also appear on overseas online networks, including GB News in the UK and RT (Russia Today) International.

Before the protest was over, Jordan B. Peterson, the Toronto professor and bestselling author, invited me on his YouTube channel — 4.75 million subscribers. As a follow-up, his daughter, Mikhalia Peterson, interviewed me for forty-five minutes on her separate channel. Gad "The Gadfather" Saad, the popular Montreal host of *The Saad Truth*, had me on for forty-five minutes. Those were the big Canadian shows but there were many others with loyal followings, including *The Andrew Lawton Show*, with True North reporter Lawton, and *The Same Drugs*, with host Meghan Murphy.

The social-media feeds, podcasts, and cable shows helped generate buzz. They got other Twitter influencers and podcasters talking about the convoy. Elon Musk tweeted several times to his 70 million followers. Joe Rogan talked about it. The UK podcast *Lotus Eaters* devoted several shows to it. So did Tim Pool, the former Vice reporter, now one of the most popular political commentators on YouTube. U.S. political commentator Jeremy Hambling, host of *The Quatering*, talked about why he would "no longer ever, ever, ever promote, or give one single cent, to anyone who uses GoFundMe," after the company called the Freedom Convoy demonstration an "occupation."

In Canada, the Freedom Convoy easily ranked as the biggest news story of the pandemic. Globally, it was the biggest Canadian story since Prince Harry and Meghan Markle announced, just before the pandemic, that they would move to British Columbia — temporarily, as it turned out. The protest made a huge story, with the most dramatic episodes yet to come.

Chapter 12

Trudeau Sets his Ducks in a Row

Prime Minister Trudeau's first public statements about the opening weekend came at a video news conference Monday morning. His "undisclosed location" turned out to be the prime minister's secondary official residence at Harrington Lake, outside Ottawa in Quebec. He walked out of the house to a porch stacked with chopped firewood and down three steps to a waiting podium. He squared his shoulders. The camera zoomed in. He opened with a ten-minute statement, then took questions for twenty minutes.

"Hate can never be the answer," he said in his prepared address. "Over the past few days, Canadians were shocked and frankly disgusted by the behaviour displayed by some people protesting in our nation's capital. I want to be very clear. We are not intimidated by those who hurl insults and abuse at small business workers and steal food from the homeless. We won't give in to those who fly racist flags. We won't cave to those who engage in vandalism, or dishonour the memory of our veterans."

He then seemed to liken the truckers' arrival in Ottawa to Russia's threatened invasion of Ukraine. "Tonight, I'll be virtually addressing the House of Commons about the situation in Ukraine," he said. "I'll be talking about the importance of freedom and democracy and the rule of law in the face of Russian provocation. In this difficult time, more than ever, we must stay true to our values, to who we are as Canadians."

As he spoke, Trudeau did his best to look grave and prime ministerial, declaiming his words like Winston Churchill rallying the British public against Nazi Germany. Repeatedly, he characterized the Freedom Convoy as a hate group. Five times in his statement, and three more times answering questions, he used the words "hatred," "hateful," and "hate," as in "symbols of hatred," "hateful rhetoric," and "intolerance and hate." He spoke of "racist flags" and "racist imagery." He cited "swastikas" and "Nazi symbolism." He repeated his "fringe minority" slur. "While this fringe minority is protesting," he said, "the vast majority of Canadians are thinking... the way out of the pandemic is... getting vaccinated."

He condemned the protesters' alleged misconduct. They had desecrated the war memorial, vandalized the Terry Fox statue, stolen food from the homeless, rejected science, rejected sacrifice, and rejected democratic principles. The "few people gathered in Ottawa right now," he said, have been duped by online conspiracy theorists "about microchips and God knows what else that goes with tinfoil hats." In answer to one question, without explaining himself, he said "There is a right to protest, not a right to shut down our democracy, our democratic processes."

Judging by their questions, reporters appeared taken aback by the hard line. Trudeau had spoken not one conciliatory word, and when reporters challenged him he conceded no ground.

"Will you meet with them or negotiate with them in any way…?"

"My focus is standing with Canadians…"

"Is there a reason that you can give as to why you will not discuss, or have any negotiations, with this particular group…?"

"Canadians know where I stand…"

"What are you going to do to appease the anger…?"

"The way out of this pandemic is getting vaccinated…"

"Is it right to paint all protesters with the same brush…?"

"There's always a right to protest peacefully…. There is not a right to incite violence, to perform acts of violence, or to spew hatred…"

It was a vicious performance and it was only the beginning. Publicly, Trudeau began setting his ducks in a row. The next day, Tuesday, during a sleepy tabling of motions in the House of Commons, several Liberal members took turns condemning the Freedom Convoy. They rose separately but in an apparent coordinated effort. One MP tabled a motion to say "that the House deplores the use of Nazi and antisemitic symbols in demonstrations on Parliament Hill." Another urged the House to "view the display of racist flags in Ottawa this weekend as shameful and a testament to the divisive and hateful rhetoric of the protest." Some of the attacks were new. A third MP, without offering evidence, demanded that the House "agree that harassment, transphobia, and all forms of homophobia seen this weekend are an insult to truth and our democracy." A fourth, again without evidence, asked that the House "condemn the display of hateful and harmful Islamophobic rhetoric by protesters on the streets of Ottawa on the National Day of Remembrance of the Quebec City Mosque Attack."

Nobody in the nearly empty House of Commons stood to oppose any of the motions. The Conservative caucus was preoccupied, getting ready the next day to dump party leader Erin O'Toole. All the declarations passed unanimously and Trudeau announced them on Twitter. Again, he sounded like Hillary Clinton railing against the "basket of deplorables."

"Today," Trudeau posted, "Members of Parliament unanimously condemned the antisemitism, Islamophobia, anti-Black racism, homophobia, and transphobia that we have seen on display in Ottawa over the past number of days. Together, let's keep working to make Canada more inclusive."

Later in the week, an additional controversy hit the news. Two men were caught on security video starting a fire in the vestibule of a high-rise apartment building and taping the doors shut. A witness, after struggling to cut the tape, put out the fire. Jonathan Kay, former editor-in-chief of *The Walrus* magazine, expressed skepticism that the arson attempt had anything to do with the Freedom Convoy.

"The story here is that last night there was a mass murder plot in an Ottawa apartment building, with one of the would-be killers telling a passer-by — for no apparent reason — he was a protestor," Kay wrote. "But no one calls 911, & Ottawa arson's unit finds out about it on twitter a day later."

Kay didn't buy the convoy connection but public officials did. The arson attempt became the seventh bogus scandal of the demonstration.

"This horrific story… clearly demonstrates the malicious intent of these protesters occupying our city," Ottawa Mayor Jim Watson said.

"Violence," NDP Leader Jagmeet Singh said of the protest, "is commonplace. We saw an example of this violence, an attempted arson downtown of an apartment building."

The demonstrators attempted "to commit arson in buildings where people were asleep," said former RCMP commissioner Bev Busson, a Trudeau-appointed senator. "These occupiers are by definition anarchists. They are professionally led, well-funded, and skilfully planning the downfall of democracy."

A few weeks later, Ottawa police caught both suspects, charged them with attempted arson, and established they had nothing to do with the Freedom Convoy. The accusation was false. Even after the truth came out, however, Public Safety Minister Marco Mendicino tried to repeat the claim to a Parliamentary committee, until Conservative MP Glen Motz called him out.

"When people who live in apartment buildings find that their front doors are locked and that fires are set in the hallways and corridors — " Mendicino started to say.

"Point of order, Mr. Speaker," Motz interrupted. "That statement right there has been proven false by the Ottawa police service and there is no connection to the protestors whatsoever, and for this minister to suggest that is absolutely unacceptable."

Chapter 13

The Conservative Leader
Gives an Interview

Erin O'Toole, leader of the Conservative Party of Canada and of Her Majesty's Loyal Opposition, didn't know what to make of the convoy. Individual Tory MPs had come to truck-stop rallies along the route to mix with drivers and declare support. In Ottawa, reporters naturally asked O'Toole if he would meet the truckers, too.

He waffled. He dodged every question. He didn't walk away or say "no comment," but he never gave an answer that anybody could understand. As soon as he won the Conservative leadership five months into the pandemic in 2020, he avoided any position that could be perceived as outside conventional opinion. He kept criticism to a minimum. He was no Nigel Farage, no Alexei Navalny. The government, O'Toole would say tepidly, should do better to ensure a made-in-Canada supply of personal protective equipment. The government should make rapid antigen tests more widely available than they are. He refused to challenge Liberal COVID-19 orthodoxy, helping to give the Freedom Convoy nationwide traction. Five days before the truckers were due in Ottawa, O'Toole also made a television appearance that resembled a late-night comedy sketch, a satire of the obfuscating politician.

"Does the Conservative Party support the mandate that requires cross-border truckers to be vaccinated, yes or no?" asked Evan Solomon, host of the CTV news show *Power Play*. The question could not have been more direct, but O'Toole began a long ramble.

"We put forward a plan on this almost a month ago, Evan, that you can support vaccines but you can also make sure you address the supply-chain shortage," the leader said. "What's disappointing, Evan, is a couple of years ago, before we had vaccines, we hailed truckers, we hailed grocery store workers, those essential workers, as heroes, and now we've allowed our debate on these issues…"

He prattled on. Solomon let him talk until he was finished.

"Okay," the host said, taking another stab. "You would reverse the vaccine mandate for cross-border truckers, is that fair to say? You would reverse the vaccine mandate?"

"What I said three weeks ago, Evan, and you know, you covered the press conference — "

"But what are you saying today?"

"[inaudible]… everybody to get vaccinated, but we can also address the supply-chain shortages without 10,000 pink slips…" He blathered on about inflation, grocery bills, lockdowns, and how Trudeau was dividing the population.

"Okay," Solomon said calmly, not losing his cool, as though playing the straight man in the comedy routine. "I'm just trying to figure out who people should listen to in terms of your party.... [Do] you believe the mandate is punishing truckers and contributing to food shortages? Is that the Conservative Party's position?"

"We need solutions to actually get products on shelves and not have tens of thousands of people lose their home, lose their livelihood, Evan," O'Toole said as obtusely as before. He went on about vaccination rates, the cost-of-living crisis, and the supply-chain shortage.

"These truckers are going to come," Solomon said firmly. "Will you go out and support these truckers when they arrive in Ottawa?"

"As I said three weeks ago, Evan, we've been meeting with industry for the last two months and I will continue to meet with industry..." He talked of people's jobs and livelihoods, and their need to be heard and not vilified.

"I'm just trying to get a straight answer," Solomon said evenly. "I know you're talking about what you said three weeks ago. I'm just asking you today.... Do you support getting rid of the border mandate, yes or no?"

"Evan, three weeks ago, as you know, I proposed a different solution, other than the mandate, to tackle the supply-chain shortage..."

At that point, Solomon must have known O'Toole would never answer the question. Nevertheless, the host plugged away, maybe to show viewers he was trying his best, or maybe to emphasize the absurdity of the exchange.

"Okay, if the truckers show up on Parliament Hill, sir, will you meet them, yes or no?"

"We've been meeting with them for the last few months and I will continue to meet this week and into the weekend with truckers and with the industry, both individual people [inaudible] but also the industry — "

"But I'm talking about the convoy…"

" — which would actually tackle the supply-chain problem. Mr. Trudeau is making inflation worse…"

Finally, even the forbearing Solomon had had enough and changed the subject.

O'Toole never did meet the truckers in Ottawa, but the day before the official arrival he ventured to the Vankleek Hill truck stop, ninety kilometres east of the capital, and spoke to a few truckers there. "I wanted to talk to some people that were actual truckers," he told a reporter in his milquetoast way, "protesting and using their democratic right."

Unlike O'Toole, core members of the Conservative Party recognized a major political development when they saw one and, even before the trucks arrived, broke ranks.

"I am in Ottawa awaiting the trucking convoy," Alberta MP Martin Shields posted the day of the Evan Solomon interview. "The Trudeau Liberal government's mandates and freedom-curbing restrictions have gone on too long."

"We oppose the mandatory vaccine on Canadian truckers," Deputy Conservative Leader Candice Bergen posted a day later. "Our economy needs to be reopened, and we need every sector working in order to recover from the pandemic. I support peaceful demonstrations against these mandates, and [I support] our truckers."

Conservative MP Leslyn Lewis mingled with the truckers when they first arrived in Ottawa and didn't shy away from reporters interested in speaking with her. "This is what democracy is all about," she told Andrew Lawton of True North. "People believe that the government has overstepped with mandates, and they're here to exercise their democratic right. We give — the people give — the government the power to act in accordance with their values. The government does not have any independent power. It is we who confer the power on the government, and, where they overstep, the people have a right to voice their opinions.... All I've seen here is loving, law-abiding Canadians expressing their voice, which they are entitled to do."

Conservative Finance Critic Pierre Poilievre served coffee to the protesters the first day. When the trucks were still on the road, he also stopped to talk to a CBC reporter about the truckers as he entered a caucus meeting.

"What do you think of the extreme elements trying to latch on to the truck convoy?" the reporter asked. It was a loaded question but Poilievre casually turned toward the microphone, his coat open to the extreme cold, his white shirt and tie showing, his every breath exhaling a stream of vapour.

"Well, you know what I think is interesting," he said, "when there's a left-wing protest on Parliament Hill, we don't see the liberal media going through every single name of the people who attend, to try to find one person that they can disparage the whole group with. The CBC, for example, has been accused by its own employees of systemic racism, and yet we don't see the media here generalize that everyone who works at the CBC is a racist.

"Whenever you have five or ten thousand people who are part of any group," Poilievre continued thoughtfully, "you're bound to have a number who have or say unacceptable things, and they should be individually [held] responsible for the things they say and do, but that doesn't mean we disparage the thousands of hardworking, law-abiding, and peaceful truckers, who quite frankly have kept all of you alive the last two years, by filling your grocery shelves with the food that you eat and filling your homes with the products that you rely upon."

O'Toole's leadership was doomed. His caucus was in open revolt. If the Conservative leader had walked out to Wellington Street and chained himself suffragette-like to the grill of a long-haul rig, vowing to stay until the cross-border mandate was lifted, he still could have never recovered. On the day of Trudeau's news conference from Harrington Lake, thirty-five Conservative Party MPs signed a letter demanding a leadership review. Two days after that, caucus members voted 73–45 to dump O'Toole. He was gone. As interim leader, the caucus elected Candice Bergen and scheduled a leadership convention for the fall.

Chapter 14

The Police Chief Talks Safety and Freedom

As the truck convoys rolled toward Ottawa at the end of January, Peter Sloly watched with anxious anticipation. He was a former deputy police chief from Toronto who, five months before the pandemic, took the top job at the Ottawa Police Service. His new mission proved relatively quiet at first. One of his toughest cases came when an officer pulled over a black man for expired licence plates, and the plates turned out to be valid. The motorist alleged racism, the officer apologized, and Sloly sent the entire staff to unconscious-bias counselling.

The Freedom Convoy would challenge him on an entirely different scale. On Friday, the day before the official arrival, Sloly briefed city officials on what to expect. If he was nervous, he didn't show it. He appeared calm and in charge, like a man who knew what he was doing. He wore black-rimmed glasses and consulted prepared notes that he held authoritatively between his hands. The police would fulfill two overriding duties at the demonstration, he told the video meeting, carried live on the internet. First, they would allow citizens to exercise their right to protest government policy. Second, they would do everything they could to maintain public safety.

"The heart of Canada's democracy is our Charter of Rights and Freedoms, the right to demonstrate and to have our views heard peacefully," the police chief said. "Public safety is paramount in all such demonstrations and will be in this demonstration, the safety of all the demonstrators, the safety of the city, the community, the residents, the tourists, and the businesses, the safety of the police officers, along with our emergency services and city of Ottawa partners."

The police would serve and protect. That was his framework. If demonstrators succeeded in expressing their views freely, without violence or breach of public safety, the Freedom Convoy could be deemed a success.

In other jurisdictions along the convoy routes, police were reporting no problems on the roads or at truck-stop rallies, Sloly said. Nobody could predict, however, what a massive, concentrated gathering might bring. Nobody knew how many trucks to expect. Maybe 1,000, he said. Maybe 2,000. He was in constant communication with key Freedom Convoy organizers, who assured him of their peaceful intentions, but there could be other groups not in touch with police, and there could be lone-wolf actors. Residents must prepare themselves. For the next couple of days, residents would be best to avoid downtown. Disruptions might continue all weekend and possibly into early the next week. Anybody who needed to shop downtown, do so now. Anybody with an appointment downtown on the weekend, think about rescheduling. Such a large crowd could have an "ever evolving fluid and dynamic nature," he said. Police were prepared for "a spectrum of risks, threats, and variables."

After the first weekend, Sloly must have felt relieved. All had gone well. The truckers and their supporters had swamped the downtown almost without incident. If there had been tensions, the police had deescalated them successfully, or the demonstrators had.

On Monday, however, the trucks were still there. They hadn't left after the weekend. At his news conference, Prime Minister Trudeau vilified the demonstrators and made clear he would not negotiate. On Tuesday, Liberal MPs in the House of Commons further maligned the throng. On Wednesday, as if in response, the truckers made themselves at home. They inflated bouncy castles and unpacked Lego blocks in front of Parliament to amuse the children. They cleared snow in front of the Supreme Court of Canada and played ball hockey. They set up pizza ovens near the Canadian Archives, next to a truck stocked with boxes of potato chips and packages of toilet paper to give away. With power drills, they assembled a plywood shack to serve as a pop-up community kitchen at Confederation Park, opposite City Hall, and along the main routes they distributed snow shovels ahead of a further snowfall. In front of the Conference Centre, temporary home to the Canadian Senate, a local enthusiast with concert speakers and DJ equipment requisitioned street space as an impromptu rave-party venue.

A city-within-a-city took shape. Supply lines improved their efficiencies. Truck neighbourhoods coalesced, and community organizations formed to ensure material security and personal wellbeing. Everybody helped each other, as they dealt with the extreme cold and the inconveniences of living day-to-day without knowing what would come next.

Beyond the downtown a broader support network grew. Local residents opened their homes to demonstrators, giving them a bed at night, or a shower when they needed one. Food arrived by the crateload. When GoFundMe announced a "review" after donations hit $10.1 million in total, supporters reverted more than ever to handing cash directly to the truckers. They passed $50 and $100 bills straight into the palms of drivers sitting in their cabs, and tossed money into bins where truckers where grilling hamburgers and cheese sandwiches. From the B.C. interior, one man phoned to ask where he could send $50,000, and sent it to a business person who had fronted money for hotels pending the release of the crowdfunded donations. Lawyers, administrators, and various other professionals stepped forward to offer expertise and share their connections.

A renewed sense of purpose infused the Ottawa team. "Our movement has grown in Canada and across the world because common people are tired of the mandates and restrictions in their lives that now seem to be doing more harm than good," Tamara told a news conference. "As of today, Sweden, Denmark, the UK, Norway, Finland, Ireland, and Switzerland have removed all COVID mandates and restrictions. We are therefore calling on all levels of government in Canada to end all COVID mandates and restrictions. We will continue our protest until we see a clear plan for their elimination."

The demonstration could never have continued as it did without broad support — particularly local support — but local anger was also growing. Ottawa had seen political rallies but nothing like the Freedom Convoy. Many residents were fed up with trucks lining the streets, honking their horns, and running their engines to keep warm. Early on, when visitors entered the downtown Rideau Centre without masks, the owners closed the mall until further notice, shutting out every retailer and shopper. In the first week, when the province allowed restaurants to reopen at half capacity, some managers declined because of noise and congestion.

Adding to the frustrations, nobody could say when the trucks would leave. Nobody with political authority would even deal with the question. Government officials might be snubbing the Freedom Convoy, but they were also doing nothing to address the concerns of angry residents. As Chief Sloly did his best to maintain public safety and to let people protest, presumably he expected the politicians to work to resolve the issues. The politicians, however, were leaving the demonstration to the police. The prime minister, the deputy prime minister, the public safety minister, the minister of emergency preparedness — all had vanished. Eventually, on Wednesday, Day Five, fresh out of his self-imposed quarantine, Trudeau emerged only to say that neither he nor his ministers would directly intervene.

"We will continue to work with law enforcement agencies to ensure that people are protected and to ensure that this protest, which is now becoming illegal, does come to an end," he told the House of Commons in French. He did not explain how the protest was going from legal to "becoming illegal."

All eyes now turned to Chief Sloly. With nobody exercising political leadership, he would have to deal with the polarized city on his own. He had prepared himself to deal with anger from the demonstrators, which hadn't materialized. He had not prepared himself to deal with anger from local residents.

Chapter 15

A Political Issue Demanding a Political Solution

On Wednesday, Day Five, with the trucks settling in, the mayor and city councillors summoned Sloly for an update. Ottawa Mayor Jim Watson spoke first.

"As you know, residents are frustrated and fed up," he said via video conference, streamed online. Residents are "frightened and angry." The police are to be commended. Such a mass protest with no deaths and no serious injuries is a "victory." The demonstration, however, cannot continue. "I want to reiterate that the symbols and acts of hate witnessed over the last several days are disgusting and do not align with the values of our community," the mayor said, parroting the disinformation from the prime minister and the corporate media. "We stand with those who continue to be affected by the displays of antisemitism, racism, bigotry, homophobia, hate, and we remain united in our condemnation of this intolerance."

Diane Deans, a city councillor and chair of the Police Services Board, spoke of "absolutely unacceptable" behaviour and lawlessness. Using military language, she called the demonstration an "occupation" and labelled the truckers "mercenaries," meaning they drove to Ottawa for the crowdfunded donations. "I want to ask the mayor if he will pick up the phone and call GoFundMe in the States directly and demand that they cease and desist sending money to these unlawful protesters," she said. "Perhaps while he's at it, he can pick up the phone and ask the prime minister to do the same."

Sloly repeated some of the complaints. "This demonstration has been intolerable, unprecedented," he said. "The range of illegal, dangerous, and unacceptable activities is beyond the ability to list in the time that we have here today, and it has had an immeasurable impact on your lives, your families' lives, the business livelihood of this city. Residents have been the victims of intense noise, threatening behaviour, hateful vitriol that has no place in our city or anywhere in our country."

Whether he believed what he was saying was hard to tell. Like others at the meeting, Sloly gave no examples of "threatening behaviour" or "hateful vitriol," and he did not add to the initial list of bogus scandals about monument desecrations and racist flags. Instead, he changed the subject, twice suggesting that ending the protest might not be a police matter.

"The longer this goes on, the more I am convinced there may not be a police solution to this demonstration," he said. "There are police chiefs, commissioners, across this country that are dealing with demonstrations that are starting, underway, and significantly advanced. This is a national issue not an Ottawa issue."

A political demonstration demands a political solution, he seemed to suggest. The prime minister might want to talk to the convoy leadership. He, or a representative, might want to listen to their side, explain the reasons for federal policy, and lay out the conditions under which the mandates could be lifted. Both parties might agree on some points. At the very least, Trudeau could tone down his rhetoric and stop calling the hundreds of thousands, maybe millions, of Freedom Convoy supporters a "fringe minority." He could stop giving Canadians reasons to keep the protests alive. Or maybe Sloly was suggesting a military solution. "We're looking at every single option, including military aid to civil power," he said, but "that option would come with massive risks."

Ordering the army to quell civil unrest has happened only twice in Canada, both times in Quebec. In October 1970, Prime Minister Pierre Trudeau, Justin Trudeau's father, invoked the War Measures Act, suspending civil liberties in response to what he called an "apprehended insurrection." Members of the militant separatist group, Front de Libération du Quebec, or FLQ, had planted terrorist bombs in mailboxes in Montreal and kidnapped British diplomat James Cross and Quebec Deputy Premier Pierre Laporte. A day after the emergency powers were declared, the kidnappers strangled Laporte to death and left his body in the trunk of a car.

In September 1990, the second occasion, Prime Minister Brian Mulroney assented to Quebec's request to send troops to the Kanesatake Mohawk Reserve at Oka, outside Montreal. Oka's mayor was determined to build a townhouse complex and expand a golf course over a Mohawk ancestral cemetery. Mohawk protesters and provincial police exchanged gunfire, and a bullet from an unknown source killed Police Corporal Marcel Lemay.

What the Freedom Convoy might have in common with the other two cases, Sloly didn't say. He ended his opening remarks with a vow to end the demonstration as safely as possible. "The more this demonstration continues, the more the risks to public safety increases," he said again. "Every option is on the table to resolve this demonstration. That said — "

Here he stopped, took off his eyeglasses, looked into the camera, and said:

" — there may not be a policing solution to this demonstration."

The next day, Thursday, Day Six, Trudeau was asked about calling in the army. "One has to be very, very cautious before deploying military in situations engaging Canadians," the prime minister said, choosing his words carefully but, like the police chief, not ruling out the possibility. "It is not something that anyone should enter into lightly, but as of now there have been no requests, and that is not in the cards right now."

To the team at the convoy operations centre in the Swiss Hotel, any allusion to military intervention sounded absurd. There had been no sign of violence, quite the opposite. Nobody was proposing to overthrow the government, either, unless James Bauder's "Memorandum of Understanding" was to be taken seriously. Even Bauder was proposing a negotiated process, and on February 8, Day Eleven, he would delete the document from his website altogether. In the downtown core, police statistics showed crime to be down, not up, and in the streets the celebratory atmosphere continued. The leader of the convoy's security team, former RCMP sniper Daniel Bulford, described the team's relations with the various police forces as excellent.

"Since early last week, when I got set up in the volunteer coordination centre," he told independent news reporters at one briefing, "I've been in constant communication with police liaisons — with Ottawa police, RCMP, OPP and PPS. We've been completely open in sharing information about anything that could be security related.... My primary concern has always been the individual or small-group bad actors that are going to try to tarnish the reputation of what we're trying to accomplish here, and — all the police know this — our group is here for everybody, for [the police agencies] as well."

Reports on social media of people from the convoy being arrested and charged were false, he also told a separate news briefing.

"I have it on very reliable information that people from the movement were not associated," Bulford said, "and that offences related to property damage and an assault just this morning committed by agitators were witnessed and reported by a trucker and one of our volunteer security personnel.... What I have seen with my own eyes, on the odd break that I get, are truckers and supporters of the movement feeding the homeless for free, right on Wellington, filling their backpacks, truckers taking a whole trailer full of food down to the homeless shelter, maintaining cleanliness of city streets, including picking up discarded masks all over the ground, that we've come to see, centralized garbage collection, shovelling snow at the war memorial and the Terry Fox statue... and providing security for those two locations."

As far as the Freedom Convoy was concerned, things could hardly be going better. The convoy's message remained unchanged: the protests would end when the mandates ended. Until then, we would keep the party going.

Chapter 16

Live from a Ditch near Kemptville

I left Ottawa after the first weekend. My plan was to go home, edit a podcast, and on Tuesday leave for an overnight run to Upstate New York. I was to deliver a load of maple syrup to a place called Mountain Top, in the Appalachian Mountains of rural Pennsylvania. On Wednesday night, I would arrive back in Ottawa and, on Thursday morning, do a live video interview with popular American podcaster Steven Crowder, host of *Louder with Crowder*. I would do it on my smartphone in front of a logging truck stacked with timber directly outside Justin Trudeau's office.

Almost right away I fell behind schedule. I ran into delays getting the truck loaded, and when I finally got to Mountain Top the receivers had closed for the day. I had to wait until morning, and because of further setbacks they didn't finish until two in the afternoon. Then the broker got the paperwork wrong, holding me up for another hour.

From Mountain Top, I drove to Elmira to pick up another load of bottles, and they were behind schedule, too. By the time I delivered the bottles in Toronto and dropped off the truck, it was two-thirty Thursday morning. The Crowder interview was set for ten. I thought if I go to bed I won't make it in time. I'll just get in the car and drive.

Somewhere around Brockville, I was too tired to continue. I had to pull over. Usually, I can never sleep in a car, but I thought I'll just close my eyes for twenty minutes and get going again. I slept for more than an hour I was so tired. When I got away again, I felt good and was on schedule to be at the logging truck in plenty of time.

By then, the temperature was fluctuating. The day before, the daytime high had risen to plus one and now the thermometer was dipping again below freezing. On Highway 416, with sixty kilometres to go, I skidded on a patch of ice. I felt the left, rear tire slip to the right, nudging the front of the car to the left. I corrected slightly one way, then the other, trying to recover. I've had lots of driver training and a lot of driving experience. The car was slowing down and everything looked okay. In the mirror, I could see cars in the distance behind me, and to be in the clear I was edging toward the side of the road. Then I hit more ice. The car fishtailed. I steered for the shoulder, and the momentum carried me off the edge down a steep slope. The car picked up speed and I hit a tree. The airbag went off in my face, and the front, right end of the car crumpled like a Coke can.

I was fine, maybe a little dazed. A motorist stopped and reached across to shut off the ignition, because I had left the engine running. A second man pulled over in a pickup. Everybody was helpful. I had no cellphone signal because I subscribe to one of the smaller carriers, good for urban areas but not for a farmer's field outside Kemptville, which is where I was. The man in the pickup handed me his phone to call police and to get somebody from the protest to come and get me. The car was beyond repair, but my mind was on the interview. When the police officer finished his paperwork, he drove me to a Tim Hortons coffee shop at the Kemptville interchange and I logged onto their WiFi. Crowder was already introducing the segment, maybe stalling for time.

"Canada, it's a silly place," he was saying, "inconsequential, generally speaking, in comparison to — okay, we love our Canadian brethren, but you have a prime minister of the country speaking out and saying that there are certain views that are impermissible and shouldn't be allowed to be spoken or written."

Crowder was born in the United States but grew up in Montreal from three to eighteen. He has a good knowledge of Canada and possesses an American's understanding of democratic freedoms. He broadcasts from Dallas, Texas, to 5.5 million subscribers, drawing partly on his years as a stand-up comic.

"These are people who are, ironically, called Liberals," he was saying, "and these are people trying to shut down really the only peaceful mass protest that I can think of in the last half decade. There hasn't even been an injury at these Canadian protests. This has been admitted, by the way, by their own police force."

He mimicked a reporter asking a police officer if anybody was hurt.

"There could have been a really bad injury or something," [the officer replies].

"But did it happen?"

No, they just put a Canadian flag on Terry Fox and then cleaned it up."

"Oh, all right, so peaceable assembly?"

"I wouldn't go that far."

"What would you call it?"

"Oh — scary."

Crowder played two Trudeau video clips, the first from *La Semaine des 4 Julie*: "They're often misogynists, often racists … do we tolerate these people?"

The second clip was from the week before: "The small fringe minority of people who are on their way to Ottawa, who are holding unacceptable views — "

"Done," Crowder said, cutting it off. "Tyrant. Don't even want to hear the rest. 'Unacceptable views.' Done. Tyrant. Period. That's it. You've crossed the line. That's it. No leader of an allegedly free country gets to determine what is an unacceptable view — outside of actual violent crime, of course. I needed to say that. Done. That's it. You're a tyrant. He needs to be out."

Crowder was one of the first commentators to identify Trudeau's autocratic streak, but he kept the interview light. When he asked where I was, I held up a Tim Hortons coffee cup.

"Canada," I said.

We covered the main points — the QR code passport, the overwhelming response to the crowdfunding campaign, the government-owned CBC's near stranglehold on news in Canada, and Trudeau's fascination with blackface as an adolescent and young adult, including his time as a high-school teacher.

At one point, Crowder started singing "Day-O." The whole interview was pretty funny. With Tucker Carlson I looked overly serious, but this time Crowder's producer titled the segment, "Freedom Convoy Trucker LIVE from a ditch in Ottawa."

Chapter 17

Trudeau Could End It at Any Time

When I got back after the car accident and the *Louder with Crowder* broadcast, I failed to see the mayhem city officials were complaining about. It was Thursday, Day Six. The city seemed much quieter than when I left. Truck and demonstrator numbers were down, although they were expected to rise again on the weekend. After two days, the all-night horn honking had ceased, and even during the day and into the evening it had dropped from nearly continuous to merely sporadic. One trucker would give a "beep-beep," and another down the block would reply with "beep," or "beep-beep-beep." They were like dogs barking to each other on a quiet summer night in the suburbs, or like Brian Griffin, the talking dog on *Family Guy*, calling out to the neighbour's dog in spoken words instead of barks.

"Hello. Hello."

"Hello."

"Are you a dog?"

"Yes!"

"I am also a dog."

"All right!"

"Yeah!"

"A dog."

"Yeah, we're dogs."

"Dogs that live near each other."

"Hey, are you guys dogs?"

"Yeah, we're totally dogs."

"Yeah, both of us."

I checked into the Sheraton Hotel. The organizing team was spread over three sites. Some members were staying at the Swiss Hotel. Others took over a floor at the downtown ARC Hotel, four blocks from Parliament Hill. A businessman who paid for some of the rooms assigned me to the Sheraton, where Tamara and a few others were staying, one block closer to Parliament. He put me in a suite that would double as our media centre. It came with a couch, a table, and a few soft chairs. I also ordered cots for supporters to use if they had nowhere else to stay, guests who helped me keep track of what was going on, both on the streets and online. They came and went. They brought food and coffee, and I scrambled to catch up to developments.

I had only been gone three days but everything seemed different. Some kind of shift had taken place. From the road, I had been following events as best I could, but up close in Ottawa I had to work hard to get up to speed on multiple changes taking place simultaneously. We were having an impact. We had the nation's attention.

In Saskatchewan, Premier Scott Moe made nonsense of the vaccine mandates, daring to say what nobody else had said before. "Vaccination is not reducing transmission," he stated categorically in what he called a "message to Saskatchewan and Canadian truckers," released on Day One of the convoy. "The current federal border policy for truckers makes no sense. An unvaccinated trucker does not pose any greater risk of transmission than a vaccinated trucker."

There it was. The federal mandates were obsolete. Two doses of a vaccine — the federal requirement — had been found to offer little protection against infection and transmission in the case of the Omicron variant, by then the dominant strain. A vaccinated trucker could get infected and spread the virus as easily as an unvaccinated one. The same went for air travellers, train passengers, and federal civil servants. Two doses of a vaccine might help avoid hospitalization and death, Moe said, but the federal rationale for separating the two groups based on transmission rates no longer applied. Moe also praised the truckers.

"Not much was known about this type of coronavirus during the early days of the pandemic," he said, switching pronouns as he went. "Truckers stepped up and kept on hauling. They crossed provincial borders and they crossed the U.S. border. You did this prior to rapid tests, prior to early intervention treatments, and prior to vaccines. You took the necessary precautions, you kept yourselves and those around you safe, and you delivered the things the people of Saskatchewan needed to live."

The premier also made clear he supported vaccines, but said he would soon end Saskatchewan's proof-of-vaccination policy, because it made no sense, just as the federal cross-border mandate for truckers made no sense. All the mandate did was "pose a significant risk to Canada's economy and to the supply chain in our Saskatchewan communities," he said.

Theresa Tam, Canada's chief public health officer, would eventually confirm Moe's central point. More than a month and a half later, she would tell a news conference that two vaccine doses offered "low" to "very low" protection against Omicron infection and spread, while still offering protection against hospitalization and death. Tam would not say the federal mandates were nonsense, but said federal restrictions were under review and might soon be lifted. They weren't.

In Quebec after the first weekend, Premier Francois Legault withdrew his idea to tax the unvaccinated. "My role as premier is to bring Quebeckers together," he said. With declining infections and hospitalizations, a previously announced staged reopening of the province also began. Restaurants reopened to half capacity, with closing time set for midnight. The blanket ten o'clock curfew was gone. Private indoor gatherings of up to four people, or two family bubbles, were permitted. Restrictions were set to ease further on February 7 for places of worship, entertainment, and sports venues.

In Ontario, as previously announced, controls were also beginning to ease, not that the Ottawa demonstrators were following them anyway. Restaurants, gyms, and cinemas reopened to half capacity. Larger venues reopened to half capacity or 500 people, whichever was fewer. Limits on indoor meetings increased from five people to ten, and the cap on outdoor gatherings rose from ten to twenty-five (not 18,000). Restrictions would be eased further on February 21, and most would be removed in March, but the changes had nothing to do with the protest, Premier Doug Ford said. He had been "extremely disturbed" to hear about Nazi flags and monument desecrations. The truckers should go home, he said, and "let the people of Ottawa get back to their lives."

In Alberta, a spinoff drama was unfolding. Inspired by the Freedom Convoy, 100 regional truckers blocked the border with Montana at the Alberta town of Coutts. They started on Saturday, the same day as the Ottawa protest, and were making the same key demands: retract the cross-border vaccine mandate and QR code. They were letting some traffic through, easing the blockade, but soon a sister protest developed twenty kilometres north at Milk River.

"This blockade must end," Premier Jason Kenney said the next day in a written release. Border crossings fell within federal jurisdiction, but highway blockades also violated the Alberta Traffic Safety Act and Alberta's Critical Infrastructure Defence Act. On Tuesday, Kenney held a news conference to elaborate.

"I hear you," he said, meaning the Coutts protesters. "Not only do I hear you but I agree with you." He had spent the weekend at the National Governors' Association annual meeting in Washington, D.C., he said, to lobby U.S. governors on several issues, including an end to the cross-border vaccine and quarantine requirements. "I certainly didn't meet a single governor who was supportive of the Canada-U.S. policy with respect to the quarantine requirement for cross-border truckers," the premier said, "and I received assurances from many of my colleagues that they would be raising this with the U.S. federal administration."

Kenney supported the truckers' demands but repeated that the protesters must end the blockade. They must reopen the border to imports and exports between the two countries and to other traffic. The Canadian Manufacturers & Exporters organization estimated two-way trade at the crossing to be $15.9 billion a year, or $44 million a day. Facing down the RCMP, the truckers refused to move. Independently, other Freedom Convoy sympathizers scheduled protests in front of legislatures in Victoria, Edmonton, Regina, Winnipeg, Toronto, and Quebec City.

In Ottawa, the establishment media continued to portray the truckers in scandalous terms. They played up the city councillors' complaints and Sloly's comments about "illegal, dangerous, and unacceptable activities." In my own interviews, I talked about the other Freedom Convoy, the one I was seeing and experiencing. I could have been talking about a Grateful Dead concert.

"How does it feel to be in the thick of something?" Dave Rubin asked on his show, *The Rubin Report*, with 1.7 million subscribers. "Canadians are not used to being in the thick of a true cultural-political moment."

"The morale on the ground is great," I said. "There's people dancing, meeting, falling in love. It's like a hippie party. We've become hippies."

"We're playing the videos, man. All the music and they're cleaning up after themselves and shovelling snow. It's awesome."

"We've had some communications with the police," I said, "because we do have a command centre with ex-military and a couple of ex-police officers there, ensuring that we have safety protocols [and that] emergency vehicles can get through. What the [Ottawa] police have indicated to us — they were monitoring us for several days — they said, 'All right, you guys have been peaceful. You've been great. We know all that stuff in the media is complete lies. Keep it up. We are not going to act. This is now a political issue, and the government will deal with you.'"

If Trudeau wanted to deal with us, I said, he could end the protest at any time. "It's the easiest win in the world for him," I said. "[He can tell us], 'You know what, I disagree with [you, the

106

truckers] but the science has changed. We're going to follow the European Union and the UK and we're going to remove all the restrictions.' Will he? I don't know."

"Right," Rubin said, "because it's hard once you've called everybody a bunch of racists, bigots, [and] homophobes."

Podcaster Meghan Murphy, host of *The Same Drugs*, asked me if I knew the convoy would grow as strong as it did. She is the Vancouver feminist known for championing exclusivity in women's changerooms, women's prisons, and women's shelters in the face of demands for inclusion by transgender women. Twitter banned her. When she gave a talk at the Toronto Public Library in 2019 about gender rights, hundreds of protesters hollered at her from outside, and Mayor John Tory criticized the library for inviting her in the first place. She left Canada to live in Mexico and talked to me from there for more than an hour.

"I had given up, I was super cynical, I was done with Canada," she said. "I was so frustrated at how passive people were being around the COVID response and all these restrictions and mandates, and I definitely didn't think anybody was going to fight back, not in a way that would make a difference, with this many people. Did you?"

"I had a suspicion that this could really have legs," I said. I told her about my trip to Alberta and Saskatchewan with Tom Quiggin a few months before the pandemic, how we spoke to a lot of people and could see how frustrated they were, especially with federal energy policy and Ottawa's anti-oil attitude.

"These are strong people," I said. "The jobs they do are tough, they are manual labour, all hours of the day, starting early in the morning, working outside when it's minus twenty degrees. There is a certain level of what we used to call 'grit' that these people have.... At the same time the truckers, generally, they're not poor people, they're middle class, so they are the voting base politicians want… and they are willing to fight for themselves, so they are the perfect group to be the first ones to take the mantle."

RT (Russia Today) International asked me about the Nil Köksal's interview with Public Safety Minister Marco Mendicino.

"CBC had a story," the host said, "suggesting that Russians were behind this and that the Americans were… funding the protests for their own goals."

I burst out laughing. I couldn't help it.

"I saw you just laugh at that," the host said. "Is that how these reports have been received?"

"Yes," I said, still laughing. "I really don't care about the fake-news media that need government money to keep sustained and that don't have an audience."

That same day, an entire week after the Köksal interview aired, the CBC issued its "clarification," essentially retracting its theory about Russia manipulating the truckers into an anti-mandate protest.

Chapter 18

Surge and Contain

"Make Ottawa boring again," somebody tweeted, half-joking. Residents exasperated with the trucks wanted their sedate, government town back. "The town that fun forgot," they sometimes called it affectionately. Pressure on Sloly was building. On the eve of the second weekend — Friday, February 4, Day Seven — he knew that Trudeau would stay on the sidelines and that the mayor and city council expected him to make the protest go away. He was still chief of police, but now he also had to be a stand-in politician. Rising to the occasion, he convened a news conference packed with local and Parliamentary reporters to announce a tough, new plan.

"Ottawa residents are frustrated and they are angry," he began, Trudeau-like, reading from a prepared text. "They have every right to be. Their lives continue to be severely impacted by unlawful and unsafe events on the city streets in the downtown core and in the downtown neighbourhoods. This is unacceptable. This morning we have begun implementing a new surge-and-contain strategy in our downtown core."

Sloly did his best to appear energized and in command. He looked down at his typed pages and up at his audience, sometimes glanced around the room, and occasionally shifted his weight lightly from one foot to the other. He outlined his three-part plan. First, the surge. In the Centretown, Lower Town, and Byward Market neighbourhoods, he would put a police officer at every intersection, a total of 150 officers monitoring the streets twenty-four hours a day. "This surge will deliver a clear message to the demonstrators," he said. "The lawlessness must end. The focus of these officers will be on acts of mischief, hate, harassment, intimidation, and other threatening behaviours."

Second, the containment. Sloly wanted to prevent an influx of vehicles that weekend, especially into the streets nearest Parliament, an area he called "the Red Zone." Police would block access to those streets with concrete barriers and heavy equipment. If a trucker were to leave for work, no outside trucker would be allowed to take the spot. Comings and goings would be closely watched. Interprovincial bridges, major arteries, and highway off-ramps would be closed and reopened as necessary. Any trucks that attempted to run the blockades would be targeted and ticketed, and police would attempt to remove them "as best we can," Sloly said.

Third, intelligence gathering. "We now have secured fully national, provincial, and local intelligence agencies," Sloly said, continuing to read from his script. From this point on, he sounded less like a local police chief and more like an emissary from the Prime Minister's Office. He kept calling the protest "unlawful." He didn't say "illegal," the word Trudeau would soon adopt, but he wouldn't say what he meant by "unlawful," either. Maybe he meant the truckers were breaking municipal bylaws by parking illegally and honking their horns. He issued a threat. Truckers might not get a ticket now, but police would keep track of all transgressions and go after offenders in the coming weeks and months, however long it took. Truckers could run but they could not hide.

"We have increased [our] ability to identify and target protesters, and supporters of protesters, who are funding and enabling unlawful and harmful activity by the protesters themselves," he said. "Investigative evidence-gathering teams are collecting financial, digital, vehicle registration, driver identification, insurance status, and other related evidence that will be used in prosecutions. Every unlawful act, including traffic and insurance violations, will be fully pursued regardless of the origin at any time in the future. The primary focus of each of these measures will be on the unlawful behaviour connected to the ongoing demonstrations,"

In response to a reporter's question, Sloly emphasized one other particular detail. "We will hold to account not just the demonstrators," he said, "but [also] those who fund and enable the demonstrators in any way." He also characterized the demonstrators this way: "The demonstrators in the Red Zone remain highly organized, well-funded, [and] extremely committed to resisting all attempts to end the demonstration safely."

As the news conference wore on, Sloly's tough-guy persona began to slip. "People have been arrested and charged," he said, as though some hard, new crackdown were underway. Until then, police had enumerated only three specific cases: one man arrested for "uttering threats over social media," another for "mischief under $5,000," and a third for "carrying a weapon to a public meeting" (a knife and a collapsible baton). Boldly, the chief tried to add a fourth. "We have already made arrests involving individuals who were intending to [bring] and were bringing firearms to the nation's capital to be involved directly or indirectly in the protests," he said.

Firearms. Wow — that was big news, except Sloly quickly backtracked. Ottawa police had not, in fact, made multiple arrests involving multiple guns. Rather, an unspecified police force, in an unnamed region elsewhere in the country, had made one firearms-related arrest. "There were partners across the country who were able to identify one individual and interdict him before he was able to get close to the city," the chief clarified weakly. Then he refocused, trying to regain his calm, assertive stand.

"A firearm was seized, charges were laid, and he will face full prosecution including potential jail time," Sloly said firmly. "That remains for anybody in this city or in this country or in any other country who intends to bring a firearm to a lawful protest to engage in unlawful activity in any way. Do not bring weapons, do not bring firearms, do not come here to cause harm, do not come here to break the law. You will be held to account."

No gun was ever found at the protest, but freelance reporter Justin Ling couldn't let the angle drop. A few weeks later in the *Toronto Star*, he would write that "a police source" assured him that "loaded shotguns" were found in "some of the trucks." In response to the story, Ottawa police would be obliged to state that they had never found any guns, in any truck, at any time.

Repeatedly, reporters pressed Sloly about what more he would do to disperse the trucks. "People will be happy to hear there are efforts being made to stop trucks from entering the core," a CBC reporter said. "People have asked why that didn't happen last weekend."

"We cannot block off the entire city," the chief replied unexpectedly, reverting to his old self. "We cannot stop anybody who wants to bring a vehicle or conveyance into the city or walk into this city. This is the nation's capital. It is a democratic society, and we have a Charter of Rights."

In the end, angry residents who demanded shock and awe got only surge and contain. Three neighbourhoods would see more officers on patrol. Intelligence agencies would gather evidence of bylaw infractions for future prosecutions. Officers would try their "best" to remove trucks, knowing that tow-truck companies would refuse to cooperate because they supported the truckers. Air horns would keep sounding intermittently during the day, diesel fumes would continue to drift in the still, wintry air, and the Freedom Convoy would persist in dominating the downtown streets until demonstrators saw signs that Trudeau would address the mandates.

Chapter 19

Chaos at the ARC Hotel

One thing Sloly said sounded funny: "The demonstrators… remain highly organized, well-funded, [and] extremely committed." It was true that everybody was determined to end the mandates and that a steady flow of money and fuel was keeping the protest running, but "highly organized" made us laugh. Compared to a week earlier, we had come a long way, but the Freedom Convoy would never develop the central organizational structure that Sloly seemed to imply. We would remain a people's movement, with all the power and frailty of a volunteer, grassroots crusade. What started as a few truckers deciding to drive to Ottawa had burst into a nation-wide protest of flag-waving and anti-mandate solidarity, a success derived not so much from good administration as from the spontaneous, unstructured efforts of creative people acting together and inspiring others to lend a hand.

More than anybody, Chris Barber got the trucks to Ottawa. Tamara started the GoFundMe. A few days after reaching Ottawa, we incorporated ourselves as a non-profit organization, with a six-member board of directors and access to accounting and legal expertise. Tamara was named president. I was named vice-president. Essentially, however, we remained a ragtag collective. From the inside, the Freedom Convoy looked the opposite of "highly organized." It looked totally chaotic.

The day Sloly announced his surge-and-contain plan, I was going back and forth to the ARC Hotel, one too many times as it turned out. The ARC was close by. Out the front doors of the Sheraton, I took a left to the first lights, another left down O'Connor Street, and left again on Slater. Some of the organizing team had rooms on the third floor. The conference rooms on the second floor we used for board meetings and brain-storming sessions. The smallest of the rooms functioned as a lunch-and-coffee gathering spot, stocked with donated food, for informal discussions and chance encounters. The rest of the hotel was empty. A numbered company, run by people we never identified, had booked all the other floors, effectively closing them to the public, including other volunteers and supporters needing a place to stay.

One thing that drove me crazy about the ARC was the number of people trying to do my job. Maybe it was my fault for leaving for a few days. Maybe people didn't know that Tamara and I were continually phoning and texting each other and maintaining communications for the convoy. Or maybe they were just getting carried away with themselves. A heady feeling had swept through the ARC, feelings of importance and authority that many team members had never experienced before. At the street level, most of the truckers didn't even know who we were. They were busy taking care of themselves and helping people around them and paying attention to immediate details and concerns. As members of the organizing team, however, it was hard not to think of ourselves as the leaders, the talk of Ottawa, the talk of the country, the inspiration to anti-mandate protests around the world. The Freedom Convoy was at the centre of something momentous, and, at the ARC, a lot of people started to think of themselves as stars in the drama.

Some of them were just partying, which was fine. We needed partiers. Others just wanted to say "fuck Trudeau," which was all right, too. The ones who concerned me wanted to get in front of the news cameras and give their opinions on behalf of the movement. They were losing focus. Pat King calling himself a leader and ranting on TikTok was bad enough without core volunteers sending conflicting messages about who we were and what we were trying to achieve.

While I was away, Tamara held a news conference with Keith Wilson, a constitutional lawyer, and Daniel Bulford, head of our command centre. They were fine. They were on message. We wanted vaccine mandates to end, including the vaccine passport. "We will continue our protest until we see a clear plan for their elimination," Tamara said.

Others at the ARC wanted to express other ideas. One board member tried to endorse the People's Party of Canada, Maxime Bernier's populist party that has never won a seat in the House of Commons. Randy Hillier, the nuisance Ontario member of the legislature, was calling the ARC saying, "Let's have a real press conference — I know how this works." He would get people scheduling their own news conferences and lining up programs of speeches for the Wellington Street stage. Some team members wanted to put activist doctors in front of the cameras, and organize a debate about COVID-19 vaccines with Dr. Theresa Tam, Canada's chief public health officer. I said if the doctors want to say they're here for freedom of choice, great, but if they want to say they have a problem with the vaccines — no. Whether we all agree on the vaccines is not the point. The point is that we all agree on freedom.

At the ARC that Friday, Day Seven, I tried to re-stake my territory. I made myself visible. I kept telling people, "Let's focus on our goal. What's our goal? Our goal is to get the mandates dropped and the passport dropped. That's our goal."

One after another, problems surfaced that day. Long after we thought we had satisfied all of GoFundMe's questions, they kept asking more. Tamara and I holed up with other board members and a couple of lawyers to go over everything again. It was tedious, mind-numbing work. At one point, Tamara said she needed a cigarette. We both got up, other people shuffled in and out of the room, and at the door she said Candice Bergen's office called.

"She wants to meet for five minutes at the A&W."

"For a photo op?" I said.

"Sounds like it."

"Tell her no. If she wants to meet, she can come over. We'll meet in one of the rooms here off the record. No cameras. No press statements. We'll talk. What can we do to help you? What can you do to help us? That sort of thing, but we're not going to align ourselves with any political party, and we're not doing a photo op so she can say, 'Hey, I'm with the truckers, I support you, and you guys can go home now, because we'll push the government to drop the mandates.'"

"Right, I'll tell Keith," she said, meaning Keith Wilson, the lawyer.

Bergen needed the convoy to go away. That morning, Senator Dennis Patterson, a former premier of the Northwest Territories and a leader in the creation of Nunavut, had left the Senate Conservative caucus to oppose the party's support for the truckers. Other senators and MPs had sided with him and Bergen was trying to mend the rift. Wilson relayed our counter-proposal to her, but we never heard from her again. Instead, she posted a video statement on Twitter, telling the public what she likely planned to tell us at the A&W — Trudeau should do something, she wants to help, and the truckers should go home.

"I know that the people who want to end the lockdowns, and end the mandates, want to be able to go home to their families and get back to work," Bergen said, "and I know that the people in Ottawa and across the country also want their lives back and to be able to get their city back. And so today I want to say, 'Prime Minister can you please help us? Can you provide an olive branch? Can you provide some hope that these demonstrators know that they have been heard?' Conservatives want to be part of the solution.... We all want to end the protests, and we all want to end the lockdowns and we all want to get back to normal life."

After the GoFundMe meetings, I headed downstairs to meet an Australian supporter in the lounge off the main entrance. It was a bright, modern room with big windows and red-upholstered couches. People were swarming around, most of them still in their parkas and holding take-out coffees. In the corner of my eye, I saw a rabbi from the Ottawa Lubavitch Hasidim Congregation starting toward me. The Lubavitch supported the protests. They were participating in our Sunday services in front of Parliament, a detail missing from the corporate media coverage, which continued to depict us as Nazis. I don't usually make a big deal about it, but I grew up Jewish. When detractors call us Nazis and white supremacists, I feel obliged to point out that I'm not a Nazi, I'm Jewish, and Tamara is not a white supremacist, she's Metis.

The Hasidic rabbi knew I was Jewish. He was going to ask me to put on Tefillin with him while he recited morning, liturgical prayers. Tefillin are small, black, leather cubes containing Hebrew parchment scrolls inscribed with the Shema and other biblical passages. Adult men attach them with leather straps around one bicep and to the forehead, but I had to meet the Australian. Off to the side, I noticed Daniel Bordman, a journalist doing livestreams for the *National Telegraph*.

"Daniel, could you do me a favour?"

"No problem," he said, spotting what was about to happen, and he stopped to strap on Tefillin for the rabbi.

Sometime that afternoon, without warning, GoFundMe cancelled our account. The donations for the truckers were gone. Worse, the platform said donations would not be refunded automatically. Donors would have to apply, and any leftover money would go to charities of the platform's choosing. GoFundMe lawyer Kim Wilford would later testify to the House of Commons public safety committee that the platform cancelled the account because of direct intervention from the Ottawa police and the mayor's office. "We heard that there were issues around violence, harassment, damage," she said. The information was false but it worked.

"I want to sincerely thank the team @gofundme for listening to the plea made by the City and the Ottawa Police to no longer provide funds to the convoy organizers," Ottawa Mayor Jim Watson posted to Twitter. "These protesters have been holding our city hostage for a week now, and I'm hopeful that limiting their access to funding and resources will restrict their ability to remain in Ottawa."

No major Canadian politician, federal or provincial, including Candice Bergen, came to the Freedom Convoy's defence. On the other hand, several powerful American leaders reacted strongly, beginning with Florida Governor Ron DeSantis. "It is a fraud for @gofundme to commandeer $9M in donations sent to support truckers and give it to causes of their own choosing," he said on Twitter. "I will work with @AGAshleyMoody to investigate these deceptive practices — these donors should be given a refund."

DeSantis was emphatic, and GoFundMe reversed itself on refunds, saying they would be automatic and immediate. That didn't stop the Florida investigation, however, and in the coming days the attorney general of Missouri would announce a similar investigation, and West Virginia's attorney general would invite residents to contact him if they had "been victimized by a deceptive act or practice" by GoFundMe.

Perhaps our strongest champion was Texas Senator Ted Cruz, who grew up in Texas but was born in Calgary.

"The Canadian truckers are heroes," he told Maria Bartiromo on her Fox News show *Sunday Morning Futures*. "Those truck drivers, God bless them, they're defending Canada, but they're defending America as well. That is courage on display, that the government doesn't have the right to force you to comply to their arbitrary mandates, and they're standing up for freedom. And, of course, big government hates it and is trying to crush them. Of course, the corporate media hates it and is trying to silence them.... People gave $10 million to support the Freedom Convoy because they were so proud of the courage of these truck drivers, and the thieves in Silicon Valley decided, 'We don't like your politics, so (a) we're going to take your money, and then (b) we're going to give it to people we like.' Listen, if anyone else did that,

that is called theft, and so today I sent a letter to the Federal Trade Commission asking that the FTC open an investigation into GoFundMe, into whether they've committed deceptive trade practices, because when people gave money, they gave money under the promise it would go to the Freedom Convoy, not to whatever left-wing political ideology GoFundMe and other Silicon Valley companies support. They are deceiving consumers and it is wrong."

At the ARC Hotel, in one of the conference rooms, a couple of board members started an account with GiveSendGo, a Christian crowdfunding site based in Boston. Money poured in. Some donors doubled their original contribution. Others gave for the first time. Within the next twenty-four hours, the fund hit $1 million. In the coming days, at a rate three times faster than the original campaign, it would surpass $10 million, almost all in small amounts from tens of thousands of supporters in Canada, and to some extent the United States and elsewhere.

I returned to the Sheraton. It had been a long day. There had been so many ups and downs. I caught up to the Sloly news conference and made an appearance on Newsmax, the online American news site. I was posting updates to various platforms when one of my group walked into the room without knocking.

"Hey," he said. "Have you seen this?"

Chapter 20

The Convoy Lawyer Makes a Video

Keith Wilson didn't like Sloly's news conference. He had arrived the day before from Edmonton, assigned by a charitable advocacy group, the Justice Centre for Constitutional Freedoms, to offer legal direction to the Freedom Convoy's board of directors. He became the board's chief counsel. After helping us with Candice Bergen, he watched Police Chief Sloly, live on the internet, lay out his surge-and-contain strategy. Afterward, without asking anybody, he decided to post a video of himself giving his reaction.

The video had a long title: "Freedom Trucker Lawyer Keith Wilson with Urgent Message from Ottawa." He looked like somebody under interrogation. He sat against a bare wall in one of the ARC Hotel's conference rooms, ceiling pot lights bouncing off his forehead like a police lamp. He was dressed in monochrome.

He wore neatly pressed blue jeans, a blue dress shirt, and a blue blazer. Speaking in a dour, steady tone, he sounded as ominous and foreboding as Orson Welles reading from *The War of the Worlds*.

"It's Friday, February 4," he said, eyeing the camera, "and I'm speaking to you from the hotel at the centre of the truckers' freedom convoy in downtown Ottawa."

The entire statement ran one minute and thirty-seven seconds.

"Over the past year," Wilson said, "the federal government in Canada, under Prime Minister Trudeau, has taken away Canadians' charter rights, constitutional rights to travel freely, has taken away truckers' rights to travel, their mobility rights, their ability to make a living under the constitution for those who've chosen to be unvaccinated.

"This afternoon," he continued, "the chief of the city police for Ottawa made announcements that are disturbing and should trouble Canadians and those around the world who support this trucker protest for freedom. The police chief essentially announced an assault on the protesters. He announced that very specific measures, that we normally only see instituted by oppressive regimes around the world, would be initiated. He effectively announced that he is going to be taking away Canadians' charter rights of peaceful assembly and freedom of expression. We are being censored."

After a theatrical pause he concluded:

"Please get this out to the world."

I put on my boots and parka and headed to the ARC. The time was just after eight. The night was cold, heading for a low of minus fourteen. A fresh, thin layer of snow covered the ground. The sidewalks were slippery. I took my time, stepping carefully.

For some reason, I brought my laptop with me, which I almost never carry around. I like to keep it in one place.

I crossed the shallow hotel lobby, mounted the stairs to the second floor, and found Wilson in a room at the end of the corridor. I had never met him. He was sitting against a bare wall under ceiling lights, exactly as he had in the video. With him were one of the accountants and a few board members, all waiting for Tamara and a couple of others to show up, and I couldn't help myself. I ripped into him.

"What the fuck did you just do?" I said. "All this doom and gloom and the world collapsing around us? I've spent the week talking about peace and love and taking the anxiety level down."

"Are you BJ?"

"The police are watching us," I said, ignoring the question. "They're evaluating our psychological reaction to Sloly's announcement. They're assessing whether we're likely to continue the protest peacefully, or turn it into something more dangerous. They're gauging our behaviour, and your video is behaviour. Trudeau took away our rights, yes. Sloly is screwing us, fine. But that doesn't have to be our future. Let's wait it out. Let's keep partying. Let's keep up the positive vibe and look to the support we see sweeping across the country."

I didn't put it that politely. I was forceful. A couple of people looked a little frightened, but Wilson started nodding. "Yes, I'm sorry, I didn't realize — " he started to say, but I kept going.

"We can't have people going off on their own, doing their own stuff," I said. "If I'm doing an interview and somebody asks, 'What's this about your lawyer saying, "Get this out to the world"?' and I haven't even seen it, if I know nothing about it, we're going to look pretty stupid. I can't say 'that was just some random guy speaking out of turn.' You're the lawyer. You're the one who's supposed to be the most careful, the most deliberate, the most measured. Red flags are going to go up. The cops are going to think, 'These people are about to try something.'"

Wilson got it. I knew that. I started to calm down. He offered to delete the video and I said it was out there now, let's leave it up, we'll deal with it. Killing it might only attract attention. People might wonder why we cut it and start speculating, which was the last thing we wanted.

"Congratulations, by the way," Wilson said. "You've just been named in a $9.8 million class-action lawsuit."

"For what?"

"For the protest."

Now it was my turn to sound out of step.

"They can't sue us," I said. "Let them sue the government."

A twenty-one-year-old Ottawa resident, a civil servant named Zexi Li, who had been complaining to authorities for days about the horn honking, was suing us on behalf of 24,000 downtown residents. Sloly's plan had not won her over. She was suing Chris Barber, Tamara Lich, Pat King, me, and sixty as-yet-to-be-identified truckers for "emotional and mental distress, difficulty concentrating, interference with quiet enjoyment of home, headaches, and difficulty sleeping." She was claiming $100 per day per resident, or $9.8 million, or approximately the total of the GoFundMe donations. Her suit would eventually balloon to $306 million.

Tamara arrived and for the next twenty minutes, speaking softly now, we laid down the law. No more video statements. No more unauthorized news conferences. I wish Sloly could have seen us. He might have changed his mind about us remaining highly organized. In the end, everybody calmed down and refocused.

Everybody would do their job and not step on anybody else's toes. Afterward, I walked carefully back to the Sheraton and got ready for bed. Then I realized I had forgotten my laptop.

By this time, it was after eleven. I started back to the ARC. The streets were quiet and empty. All the office windows were dark. Long-haul rigs were parked here and there, but the horns were silent and fresh snow muffled the few remaining city sounds. When I was almost at the hotel, in front of the Export Development Canada building, my rear foot slid on a patch of ice. The sole of the boot skidded to the right, like the back wheels of my car outside Kemptville. I tried to correct with the front foot, it slipped in the other direction, and my right ankle collapsed, then snapped.

A sick feeling swept through me. Two hours earlier, laying into Wilson, I felt assertive and in control. Now I lay sprawled helplessly on the icy sidewalk. In the shadows, in the muted glow of streetlamps covered in snow, loomed the giant trucks. The day's anxieties unspooled in my head — Sloly making his threats, GoFundMe shutting us down, Candice Bergen making her play, Wilson posting his video, Zexi Li filing her lawsuit, and the ARC team carrying on a general state of bedlam. My car was smashed, my laptop was missing, and my ankle was throbbing. Lying on the cold cement, feeling vulnerable, I could easily imagine the entire convoy demonstration careening sideways out of control.

"Hey, you need some help?"

A hundred metres away, a couple of men were standing outside the hotel having a cigarette. One of them I recognized, a volunteer with one of the groups at the ARC I had been dressing down earlier. The other was a big, burly type who could have been a trucker. They both came over.

"Are you all right?" the first one said.

"I think so," I said. "I can wiggle my toes. It's not broken." But when I tried to get up my right leg crumpled.

"Can I help you, can I help?" said the burly one, and he leaned over to put his hand on my lower leg. "Please, Jesus," he said. "Bless the Lord. Please, Jesus, heal this ankle."

"Thank you, brother, I appreciate it," I said, trying not to sound sarcastic. "How about a medic? Can we get a medic instead?"

They helped me up. Taking either side, they carried me into the lobby, and lowered me onto a red-upholstered couch next to the front door. Somebody called 911, and people who had been attacking me a couple of hours earlier gathered around with creased foreheads, expressing concern.

"Here, take this," one of them said. "It's a Percocet."

"That's good stuff," somebody else said.

I always thought if you broke a bone it would really hurt, but I didn't feel any sharp pain. Normally, I resist taking any kind of medication whether I'm in pain or not, but everybody was being nice and offering pills, so I took one.

When the paramedics arrived in an SUV, they looked at my ankle and said it was probably broken, even if I could wiggle my toes. They put it in a brace. After I recovered my laptop, somebody drove me to the hospital, and within ten minutes I was in front of a doctor. He took an X-ray, which showed both bones of my right ankle broken, the tibia and fibula. He would reset them, he said, and gave me a shot of ketamine, an anesthetic that, instead of putting you to sleep, makes you spacey and euphoric. Recreational users call it "Special K." I saw colours moving around and felt the powerful, ecstatic feelings again of Day One of the convoy. I felt like dancing on Wellington Street and demanding our freedoms back.

Chapter 21

The Police Oversight Board Demands Action

Diane Deans believed in the right to protest until the trucks arrived. She was a long-time city council member, serving her eighth consecutive term for Gloucester-Southgate Ward, in Ottawa's south end. She was also chair of the Ottawa Police Services Board, a seven-member civilian oversight body created to ensure that the police handle themselves legally and correctly, and not overstep their powers.

"We live in a democracy," she told the board three days before the Freedom Convoy's official arrival. "All people have the right to peaceful protest. We need to create space for those protesting to have their voices heard, and we need to make sure that the environment is safe for everyone, including those protesting and members of the public. It's important for public figures to lead by example, regardless of our own political beliefs."

One week into the demonstration, and one day after Police Chief Sloly announced his surge-and-contain strategy, the only surge she saw was from thousands of fresh protesters pouring into the city. As temperatures hovered at minus sixteen degrees, television reporters again described a "carnival-like atmosphere." People danced to keep warm. Supporters lit barbeques and wood fires on the snow-covered lawn of the West Block. They tended bonfires along Wellington Street, warming small gatherings of people, and distributed baked goods from portable heaters. Two horse riders appeared. One carried a Canadian flag, the other a "Trump 2024" flag. Without identifying themselves specifically, they said they were from Brantford, Ontario, and their horses were named Homer and Boony. Two other men tried to drive a chuckwagon carrying a diesel tank toward the protest site, but police turned them around.

On Saturday afternoon, Day Eight, Deans summoned Sloly to an emergency meeting. She gave him one hour's notice. In a board Zoom call, carried live on the internet, she opened with a short statement that included the words "siege," "terrorizing," "torturing," "threat to our democracy," "insurrection," and "madness."

"We are on Day Eight of this occupation," she said staring into the camera in oversized blue-framed glasses. "Our city is under siege. This group is emboldened by the lack of enforcement by every level of government. They are terrorizing our residents, torturing them with incessant honking, threatening them and preventing them from leading their lives. People cannot go to work or open their businesses. They cannot sleep, walk, shop, go to medical appointments or enjoy their neighbourhood. This group is

130

a threat to our democracy. What we're seeing is bigger than just a City of Ottawa problem. This is a nationwide insurrection. This is madness. We need a concrete plan to put an end to this now."

She put Sloly on the spot.

"Chief, in your opinion, as the chief of police in the City of Ottawa," she said, "do you believe that you are still able to provide, given the fluid situation of this occupation, adequate and effective policing to the residents of our city?"

Sloly kept his cool and turned Deans's hyperbole to his advantage.

"I think you've just, in your own wonderful words, described what my police service and I have been trying to manage on behalf of this city for eight solid days," he said, sounding sincere. "The oath of office that I and my officers swore was never intended to deal with a city under siege, a threat to our democracy, a nationwide insurrection driven by madness."

The Police Services Board was formed to stop police from getting out of line, but now the roles were reversed. Deans, chair of the civic oversight authority, was revved up, and it fell to Police Chief Sloly to rein her in. There might be no policing solution to the demonstration, he said, reiterating his point of a few days earlier. Nothing in the Police Services Act lays out how to deal with such a situation. He praised Mayor Watson for scuttling the GoFundMe donations and said the next step would be to staunch the fuel supply. He reviewed his surge-and-contain plan. The Ottawa police force was stretched to the limit, he said. All days off had been cancelled. Some officers were working twelve-hour shifts, day after day. The RCMP would be sending sixty officers — revised later in the meeting to 250 — and eight Ontario municipal forces were sending personnel: Toronto, York Region, Peel Region, Durham Region, Cornwall, Kingston, London, and

Waterloo. He was doing everything he could, but the Freedom Convoy was unprecedented. "This is something that is different in our democracy than I've ever experienced in my life," he said.

Deans didn't like what she was hearing. To her question as to whether the police chief could end the protest, "the answer I heard from you is 'no,'" she said. She wanted to stop the "mayhem." What about invoking Section 63 of the Criminal Code? she asked. The city could get a judge to declare an "unlawful assembly," which would allow the mayor to declare a riot, which would authorize the police to make mass arrests.

"We have looked at that," said city solicitor David White. "That is a somewhat archaic section. We've not actually been able to find any occasion when it's been invoked."

What about declaring a state of emergency? Deans asked.

A symbolic gesture, White said. The city and police would get no extra powers.

City Councillor Carol Anne Meehan spoke up.

"We're giving the signal to all these people coming into town that it's a free-for-all," she said, her voice rising in pitch and sounding as desperate as Deans. "They can take tires off trucks. They can put up buildings [the pop-up kitchen at Confederation Park]. They can bring in fuel. They can take over our stadium [the baseball stadium parking lot]. We've given them the signal — 'come and party in our town.'"

Meehan started pleading.

"We want to know the plan," she told Sloly. "We want to know concretely what is going to happen. Are we going to start making arrests or do we just wait for more intelligence?... Please, I'm begging you. Give us some answers. What is going to be done?"

Speaking evenly, the chief tried to lower the temperature with an analogy. "People wanted to know when there would be an end to COVID," he said. "There is no detailed plan to these things."

"We have to be the level head," Police Operations Chief Trish Ferguson chimed in, trying to help. "We still have to follow the Charter of Rights."

"Most of all," Sloly said again, "we need a solution that is beyond a police solution for something that is not a policing issue. It is a societal issue."

That gave Deans another idea. "This is an extraordinary emergency and we need extraordinary measures," she said. "We need to ask every level of government to use the powers and authorities that they have to declare the emergencies that we need to bring this situation to a peaceful ending. We cannot allow this kind of terrorism in our community to continue in this way."

"The prime minister has to make a statement," Meehan said in agreement. "[The protesters] are not going to go away until they hear from him. He can't ignore this anymore. This is in his front yard."

"I'm sorry," Deans said, contradicting her colleague, "but I'm not sure that meeting with terrorists is something that he's going to do."

"Terrorists," "terrorism," and "terrorizing." With three different parts of speech, Deans accused the Freedom Convoy of some of the most heinous behaviour possible, one that demanded a fierce police response.

Ottawa Mayor Jim Watson, who does not sit on the police board, expressed to reporters his distaste for the unauthorized fun taking place. People were dancing in the streets without a municipal permit and riding horses downtown in violation of a specific city bylaw. At the baseball stadium parking lot, they were basking in three wood-fired sauna shacks and a generator-run hot tub. "It's disturbing when you see the protest turning into what looks like some kind of fun carnival," Watson told CTV with a long face, "where they have bouncy castles and hot tubs and saunas. A complete insult to the people who are putting up with this nonsense... and it shows a great deal of insensitivity."

On Sunday, although he could cite no law against undue insensitivity, Watson declared a state of emergency. The move was little more than symbolic, as the city solicitor had told the police board. It allowed the city to secure emergency supplies, as in a flood, without going through a bidding process. A city press officer, however, put the case more dramatically: "Declaring a state of emergency reflects the serious danger and threat to the safety and security of residents posed by the ongoing demonstrations and highlights the need for support from other jurisdictions and levels of government."

The same day, police asked protesters to leave Confederation Park and they did. They hauled away their community kitchen, and, after they left, police erected fences around the area. "No arrests," Sloly declared redundantly, "no use of force, no injuries, no deaths, no riots, no encampment at Confederation Park. It is gone. We have... reclaimed that territory."

"We just request that the prime minister comes out and talks to us," demonstrator George Tiger told Global News. "We want to talk."

The same evening, police also appeared in force at the Coventry Road baseball stadium. Originally, police had directed the trucks to the stadium, and the truckers had turned the parking lot into a staging and supply area for the protest. On Sunday night, however, police seized a tanker with 3,500 litres of fuel, towed away a number of trucks, and removed the saunas and hot tub that Watson found beyond the pale.

As evidence of heightened enforcement, Sloly and Deputy Chief Steve Bell issued several updates. The number of arrests during the protests now totalled twenty, including two for "mischief" Sunday at the stadium. Police had issued 500 tickets, including 115 for parking and other traffic offences, which included driving the wrong way, driving with a defective muffler, driving without a seatbelt, and having alcohol "readily available." Police had also opened fifty criminal investigations. One was "progressing well," Bell said — the investigation into the woman dancing on the Tomb of the Unknown Soldier.

The list didn't add up to much. Announcing a seatbelt infraction seemed to be scraping the bottom of the barrel. Sloly all but admitted that the demonstrators had the upper hand. "Every time we knock something down, there are attempts for it to pop up in four or five other locations," he said. "We are rapidly deploying our resources whenever we get a sense of another fuel depot, another staging area, or anything else that enables the demonstration to continue."

He also made a fresh vow. Police will cut the fuel supply. Anybody caught trying to transport diesel or propane to the truckers would be subject to arrest. "We're going after any conveyance," Sloly said in his firm, serious way, "including horseback, people carrying jerry cans. We are arresting and seizing."

A short time later, from the stage truck on Wellington Street, a member of the organizing team asked for 200 volunteers. She directed them to the ARC Hotel, where a pickup truck pulled up towing a trailer packed with empty jerry cans. While organizers passed them out, a second pickup arrived with jerry cans full of fuel. Some volunteers would serve as decoys, others as fuel carriers. Volunteers chose their own role and formed lines to walk jauntily together past the police toward the protest. Most of the officers laughed. They got the joke. They couldn't tell who had fuel and who didn't, and they knew of no law against walking down the street with a five-litre jug anyway. As the volunteers paraded happily down Wellington Street, the red jerry can — like the Canadian flag and the children's drawings — became another symbol of the anti-mandate protest.

Chapter 22

Non-violence Gives Us the Upper Hand

We could not let the terrorism charge go answered. Diane Deans might have been melting down and not speaking rationally, but she was a prominent public official and hadn't simply misspoken. The next day, Tamara and I called a news conference for independent media at the Sheraton. I was dressed for the indoors, in a T-shirt and a pair of loose sweat pants to accommodate the cast. I stretched my right leg in front of me, my big toe poking through the plaster. Everybody else was wearing heavy shirts, hoodies, and snow boots. Tamara took the spot on the couch next to me, in the middle. On her other side sat Daniel Bulford, the former RCMP sniper. Keith Wilson, the lawyer, occupied a separate chair, and Tom Quiggin, the former military intelligence officer, perched himself to our left on the window sill.

One of the journalists live-streamed the session, making it accessible to the corporate media and everybody else. Addressing the terrorism charge, Quiggin spoke first.

"If we smell a terrorist, if we see any hint of a terrorist, if we hear two words together that might connect with political violence, the first call we make goes to the integrated national security enforcement team of the RCMP," he said. "The second call goes to the Ottawa police intelligence section. We have no information, nowhere, nothing, of anybody operating within our ranks, or even around us, who has the intention of carrying out an act of political violence."

Bulford was similarly categorical.

"They label us as terrorists and holding the city hostage — that's laughable," the former Mountie said. "I know the officer in charge of the Integrated National Security Enforcement Teams in Ottawa. We have a great relationship. Or, in the past we did. Over the last roughly four years of my time with the team here in Ottawa, I was leading an initiative to go around to senior managers of the RCMP, different units, to try to convince them [to create] a designated national counter-terrorist, hostage-rescue team. So when I hear comments that we're taking the city hostage and we're terrorists — it's ridiculous."

For the city authorities, the biggest problem wasn't that the protest was violent but that it was peaceful. Like Trudeau, they could call us names, but we had a democratic right to political protest and civil disobedience. As long as we stayed non-violent, we could keep the upper hand.

"Everybody knows this has turned out to be the biggest party, the most friendly atmosphere of a gathering of people in Ottawa's history," I told the briefing. "It's shocking some of the language that some of the elected officials in Ottawa have been using. I can't believe it, but that's their issue. We're here just trying to be positive and we're just waiting for the government [to talk to us]."

We ran through other developments. Trudeau had essentially fled the scene, leaving Sloly and Mayor Watson in charge. "A Trudeau puppet," Quiggin called Watson, a Liberal Party member and former two-term Ontario Liberal cabinet minister. His strategy was to starve us out. He had successfully sabotaged the GoFundMe account, but the GiveSendGo campaign was taking off. Over the course of the week, the operations centre had to switch from fuel trucks, to three-quarter-ton trucks, to five-litre jerry cans, but fuel was getting through. Food donations were still arriving by the crateload. The police were writing tickets to scare truckers into leaving, Quiggin said, but that angle wasn't working either.

"They don't have a strategy, they have a series of disconnected tactics," he said. "They want the streets cleared, but they have no real idea of how they want to get there."

Tow-truck companies, who were themselves truckers, were refusing to cooperate.

"A guy called from Buffalo," Quiggin told reporters. "He has a Class A towing licence [for] super heavy loads. He gets a call. Can you bring your trucks to Canada? He told them he couldn't do operations in Canada for insurance reasons. The government is calling all the way to Buffalo and they can't get anybody. No tow-truck company that wants to stay in business is going to help tow away trucks."

Three days later, on Wednesday, Day Twelve, Tamara, Keith Wilson, and I met the independent reporters again. We addressed two major developments. One was the Ambassador Bridge blockade. Inspired by the Freedom Convoy, Canadian truckers were blockading the bridge spanning the St. Clair River between Windsor and Detroit. The bridge was the most heavily trafficked land crossing between Canada and the United States, a trade route especially important to the agricultural and automotive sectors. Ontario Premier Doug Ford put two-way trade at $700 million a day in Canadian dollars.

We had nothing directly to do with the Ambassador Bridge. Nobody in Windsor had called us, and we didn't know about it ahead of time, but we were on the same side. We both wanted Trudeau to end the vaccine mandate for cross-border truckers and to cancel the ArriveCAN app. Similarly, we had nothing directly to do with the Coutts, Alberta, protest, which included an on-and-off blockade, or with border protests developing at Emerson, Manitoba, and Surrey, British Columbia. Our policy was not to block anything. We had lined the downtown Ottawa streets with trucks, but we were also working with local authorities to keep lanes open for emergency vehicles and other traffic. We were running our protest our way. We wished the other protests well.

The second development we addressed was the class-action lawsuit. Paul Champ, the lawyer representing Zexi Li in the $9.8 million case, had appeared before Ontario Superior Court Justice Hugh McLean to request an injunction against the honking of air horns and train horns. The all-night honking had stopped after the first weekend, but horns were continuing to sound during the day. Wilson told the court that, as a gesture of goodwill, with or without an injunction, the truckers would stop honking their horns. McLean issued a temporary injunction. Based on the evidence, horns were having a damaging effect on residents, the judge said, but he would limit the injunction to ten days pending further submissions. More people might wish to come before the court to testify, he said. In fact, 110 local residents had already come forward on their own to swear affidavits expressing approval of the protest.

"They have come forward wanting to swear how well behaved the truckers have been," Wilson told the news conference, "how they have been shovelling sidewalks, how it's a festive environment, and how important it is to them that the truckers are here to show their concern about the loss of freedoms and the efforts to get them back. It's been remarkable. People are usually reluctant to come forward and swear on their own initiative."

Wilson also said that over the course of the three- or four-hour hearing, the judge went out of his way on a number of occasions to make one thing "crystal clear." "[He said] these truckers have a lawful right to be here to protest. They have a lawful right to free expression, both under common law… and most clearly under the Charter of Rights and Freedoms," Wilson told the reporters. In his written decision, the judge also reaffirmed that position. "Provided the terms of this Order are complied with," he wrote, "the Defendants and other persons remain at liberty to engage in a peaceful, lawful and safe protest."

Police Chief Peter Sloly was talking about the Charter of Rights and Freedoms, and Justice Hugh McLean was not about to let anybody trample on our constitutional rights, either.

Chapter 23

Tom Marazzo Calls
a News Conference

I thought I had sorted everything out at the ARC Hotel. Team members there would do their jobs organizing the trucks, block by block, keeping everybody happy, and shepherding food and fuel supplies. I would continue as official spokesperson for the Freedom Convoy. I would do interviews with the major podcasters and continue to post updates to social media. Just when I thought everybody's role was understood, however, the boundaries collapsed again. Maybe it was the attention we were getting, or the millions of dollars in donations pouring in, or maybe it was the frustration at seeing no clear sign that the government would end the mandates and the QR vaccine passport. Either people were letting fantasies of fame and riches go to their heads, and they wanted to be superstars, or they thought if they spoke for the convoy, instead of me, they would get better results.

One day, Tom Marazzo called the independent reporters to the ARC for an announcement. Marazzo was not a member of the convoy organizing committee, or the board of directors. He was a former Canadian Armed Forces captain who, after eighteen years, retired to teach computer software development at Georgian College in Barrie, Ontario. He lost the job in 2021, he has said, when he sent an internal email to 250 faculty and staff questioning whether the college's vaccine mandate was legal. He arrived in Ottawa as a volunteer and found a role for himself as a truck manager. When I first met him, he told me, "I'm going to be like a ghost, invisible. I'm going to manage the trucks and make sure everybody is safe. I'm going to deal with everything behind the scenes, and nobody will even know I was here."

Now he was calling a news conference to speak to people "around the world, around Ontario, and around Canada." He arranged his set the way a prime minister or a provincial premier would, with himself front and centre, surrounded by senior officials, in this case convoy leaders. Brigitte Belton sat to his left, Chris Barber to his right. Tamara Lich could be seen standing toward the right of the frame. Tom Quiggin stood near the back. Activist doctors and road captains from various regions filled out the ranks, bringing the total number of people in his entourage to fourteen. Pat King was also there, streaming the session live. It was the only time I knew King to be associated with any meeting or event connected to the convoy leadership.

"This broadcast," Marazzo began, "might be called a preemptive SOS."

He was hearing rumours that police were marshalling their resources, preparing to clear the trucks and protesters from the

144

streets. Be prepared to respond, he urged his audience. Be prepared to come to Ottawa. He could offer no timeline, he said. People watching did not need to pack a bag immediately, but "start preparing your families, or start talking to your employers and saying, 'Listen, I really feel my place is in Ottawa this week.'" The moment all telecommunications go down will be the moment the police move in, he said. A media blackout will mean it's happening. That's the moment to come.

Marazzo spoke not in the doomsday-type voice that Keith Wilson used in his video, but informally, as casually as to his computer software class, with the fingers of both hands casually cupping a plastic water bottle on the desk in front of him.

"We have a room booked, twelve o'clock tomorrow," he said, still relaxed, unhurried. "I'll meet with Justin Trudeau myself. I'm prepared. We are prepared. All of us."

He urged everybody to stay calm.

"Let's find a peaceful resolution to this," he said. "I want to go home, but I'm not going until I'm no longer needed here, and, based on all the support we have from the people of Canada, I have an incredible amount of support and a lot of people that seem to want me here, and I'm not going home until the job is done."

Consistently, Marazzo said he wanted to keep the protest peaceful, then used a bullet analogy when speaking of Trudeau's brain. "He's got a .22-calibre mind in a .357 world," Marazzo said, dangerous language for somebody posing as spokesperson for a mass demonstration.

Wandering briefly off the topic of meeting Trudeau, Marazzo plunged into a variation of James Bauder's "Memorandum of Understanding," the crazed document we had rejected from the beginning. "Let's get at a table," he said.

"Enough hiding. I'm willing to sit at a table with the Conservatives and the NDP and the Bloc as a coalition. I'll sit with the governor general. You put us at the table with somebody that actually cares about Canada…. I'll talk to any level of government that can actually get a decision done, because we can see clearly the Liberals don't want to talk to us. We want to talk to them. They are the official Government of Canada, but can you just come and meet us at a table?"

At this point, if the establishment media were to ridicule us for talking nonsense, I would say they were only doing their job. Justin Ling was quick off the mark, for once using the unadorned truth to discredit us.

"In an 'emergency' press conference," he posted to Twitter, "the truckers' new spokesperson Tom Marazzo says: 'I'm willing to sit at a table with the conservatives and the NDP and the Bloc, as a coalition. I'll sit with the governor general.'"

CTV's Evan Solomon retweeted the post, adding, "The organizers repeatedly and openly show they have no interest in the democratic process or the rule of law. Not just their MOU but here the spokesperson says he's 'willing' to sit as a 'coalition' with elected MPs in government. Democracies don't work like that."

Public Safety Minister Marco Mendicino chimed in. "Most Canadians understand that there is a difference between being tired and fatigued with the pandemic," he said, "and then crossing into some other universe in which you're trying to set up a parallel structure."

Fair enough. Marazzo gave no sign of having gone rogue. He had surrounded himself with Brigitte Belton, Chris Barber, Tamara Lich, Tom Quiggin, and some of the senior road captains. Nobody could blame outsiders for thinking Marazzo spoke for the convoy. On the positive side, the scene never repeated itself. Two days later, Keith Wilson obliquely addressed the matter for the independent news media as best he could.

"I'd also like to clarify," the lawyer said. "At no time has anyone involved in the core group of the Freedom Convoy asked for anything other than that their Charter rights be restored, the rule of law in Canada be respected, and the mandates that arbitrarily discriminate against them and usurp their Charter rights be stopped. There are elements out there with different agendas talking about some fantasy, the governor general striking the government and magically appointing a committee. It's all fairy dust. It has no basis in reality, and it's nothing that anybody in this group that I work for has ever suggested, nor do they suggest it now. Their goal is for all Canadians to have their rights back, full stop."

After that, from time to time, Marazzo continued giving video statements, but he did so on his own. None of the convoy leaders sat with him anymore. A few vloggers continued to attend his sessions, and he continued to say things such as, "I will sit at a table with you, Mr. Prime Minister. I will talk to you. I will work out a deal with you." He continued to entertain grand notions about himself. Five months later, he would run as a candidate for Derek Sloan's fledgling Ontario Party in the provincial elections and take 3.77 percent of the vote in the riding of Peterborough-Kawartha. On his campaign website, he would say of his role in the Freedom Convoy: "Tom [Marazzo] acted as the main spokesman, doing almost daily press conferences on behalf of the convoy."

Chapter 24

Pierre Poilievre Proposes a Solution

On Thursday morning at six o'clock, Day Thirteen, a friend drove me to Ottawa Hospital for ankle surgery. COVID-19 protocols meant I had to enter alone, but an attendant brought out a wheelchair and steered me to the second floor. After the usual prep work, I met the surgeon. He would be screwing two plates into the bone to stabilize the break and help it heal, he said, which sounded neat and tidy, although the X-rays I saw afterward showed metal sticking into the bone from all directions.

In the recovery room, I got a lesson in pain relief. The anesthetist administered a nerve block to the right foot, freezing the leg from the knee down. When the effect wore off in twenty-four to thirty-six hours, I would feel intense pain for a couple of days, the surgeon said. He wrote a couple of prescriptions. "Don't put any weight on the foot," he also said. "None."

Being on nerve blockers and painkillers helped numb me to the ups and downs of political developments over the next couple of days. At the Ambassador Bridge in Windsor, all traffic was blocked between Canada and the United States. Nothing was getting through. A second bridge at Sarnia, to the north, was also blocked, and that morning just north of the Manitoba-North Dakota border, at Emerson, protesters in about fifty semi-trailer trucks, snowplows, tractors, and construction vehicles began blocking the highway in both directions. They were letting only medical and livestock vehicles pass. Protests also continued at Coutts and Milk River, Alberta, and on streets leading to the Pacific Highway border crossing in Surrey, B.C.

Pressure was building on Trudeau to do something. The Windsor blockade alone was affecting US$13.5 million in economic activity per hour, according to numbers from the Windsor-Essex Regional Chamber of Commerce. The auto industry, especially, was being disrupted. A General Motors plant outside Lansing, Michigan, and a Honda plant in Alliston, Ontario, announced manufacturing stoppages for lack of parts.

In a stunning break with Liberal Party orthodoxy, a backbench Quebec MP, Joël Lightbound, held a news conference to accuse his own leader, the prime minister, of deliberately politicizing vaccine mandates and Covid-19 restrictions. "A decision was made to wedge, to divide, and to stigmatize," he said, a strategy that is "undermining the public's trust in our public health institutions." He was not the only member of Trudeau's team who felt, to varying degrees, as he did, he said, and expressed a wish to "push for change from within caucus."

On Thursday afternoon, Interim Conservative Leader Candice Bergen rose in the House of Commons. This was her chance to put Trudeau on the spot. Instead, she told the truckers to go home, withdrawing her support. "I want to speak directly to Canadians who are demonstrating here in Ottawa and across the country," she said. The protesters have been heard, she assured her listeners. Conservatives will not rest until the mandates are lifted, etc. "Today, though, I am asking you to take down the blockades," she said. "It's time to remove the barricades and the trucks for the sake of the economy and because it's the right thing to do."

Bergen was a stop-gap leader, responsible for keeping Conservatives together pending a leadership vote in the fall. The Ottawa protest was dividing the caucus. From her point of view, nothing good could come from truckers remaining in Ottawa, and from other truckers expanding the protests nationally, causing unpredictable disruptions. She turned as cautious as Erin O'Toole, but that didn't mean a contender for the party leadership had to do the same.

That evening, Conservative Finance Critic and newly declared leadership candidate Pierre Poilievre posted a two-page open letter to Trudeau on Twitter. It stood out as perhaps the most powerful Opposition document of the two-year pandemic, bolder and more comprehensive than even Scott Moe's statements of two weeks earlier. Typically, the corporate media downplayed it.

The letter cited Liberal MP Lightbound's allegations. It also quoted Canada's chief public health officer, Dr. Theresa Tam, as saying mandates might have to be re-examined. "We need to get back to some normalcy," she said. In the rest of the world, restrictions were being relaxed, Poilievre said. The United Kingdom, Ireland, Norway, Denmark, Sweden, Finland, South Africa, and others had either removed them already or were in the process of doing so. The rest of the world was moving forward and Trudeau was moving backward.

"You imposed this mandate… to again divide Canadians and disparage a minority for your own political gain," he wrote. He called on the prime minister to take three specific steps. First, end all federal mandates. The move would include dropping the cross-border mandate for truckers, talking to U.S. President Joe Biden about ending his matching mandate introduced a week later, and letting unvaccinated public servants return to work. Second, convene a meeting with the premiers with a view to ending provincial vaccine passports and mandates. Third, state clearly that nobody will be taxed for being unvaccinated (as the Quebec premier had proposed).

"Do not allow your spite towards the trucker protest to stand in the way of doing the right thing," Poilievre said in closing. "Your pride and ego come after the public interest."

The next day, Ontario Premier Doug Ford declared a state of emergency. Blocking the movement of people or goods along critical infrastructure is illegal, he said. Fines for breaking such laws will be severe. The maximum penalty will be $100,000 and up to a year in prison, and the government will look into legislation to take away personal and commercial licenses, he said. The same day, the government won a court injunction freezing donations of more than $10 million to the Freedom Convoy's GiveSendGo account. None of the contributions reached the truckers.

At the announcement, Ford lumped together the bridge blockade and the Ottawa demonstration, making no distinction. He called the Ottawa protest a "siege" and an "occupation," the same misleading military-type words that Diane Deans had used.

"Siege," says *The Canadian Oxford Dictionary*, means "a military operation in which an attacking army attempts to force the surrender of a fortified place by surrounding it and cutting off supplies and communication, etc." By that definition, the City of

152

Ottawa, through its police force, was laying siege to the protesters, not the other way around.

"Occupation," the dictionary says, means "the act of taking or holding possession of (a country, district, etc.) by military force." That's not what was happening on Wellington Street. Block captains kept the lanes open until the police themselves barricaded streets to prevent trucks moving in to take a vacated spot. To the politicians, however, truth and accuracy seemed beside the point. From then on, Ford, Trudeau, and Watson repeatedly lumped all the demonstrations together, falsely characterizing the Ottawa protest as an "occupation," a "siege," and a "blockade."

Chapter 25

The Man in the Wheelchair

On Sunday, I was scheduled to speak after the religious service on the boom-truck stage. That meant walking four blocks from the hotel, not far except I was on crutches, the sidewalks were icy, and the temperature was minus twenty degrees. It was another cold, sunny, winter day. Two livestreamers helped me, Daniel Bordman and Salman Sima. One walked ahead checking for slippery patches, the other hovered alongside me. The trip took thirty minutes, but we finally arrived at the intersection of Wellington and Metcalfe Streets, the Freedom Convoy Central Square, or what I called "Trudeau's Truck Stop."

We were into our third weekend. The giant rigs now looked like part of the landscape. One of the drivers had stuck a letterbox to a post, the way a farmer does at the end of a laneway. Two men from Quebec, bare-chested and laughing, without a permit from

Mayor Watson, sat on the street in a hot tub powered by an electric generator. Everybody else was bundled up, the crowds not as thick as on opening day but the atmosphere just as festive. The momentum was still with us. Over the weekend, freedom rallies were again taking place in front of almost every provincial legislature in the country. In Canberra, Australia, a protest inspired by the Freedom Convoy grew to 50,000 people. At their request, I sent three video messages on the convoy's behalf to be played on a Canberra jumbotron. In Paris, a "convoi de la liberté" — vehicles from Lille, Perpignan, Nice, and other cities — converged on the Arc de Triomphe and the Champs-Élysées, honking their horns and waving French and Canadian flags from their windows as riot police sprayed the air with tear gas. Nationwide, the French interior ministry estimated protesters to number 32,000 people.

The service on the boom truck ended. Two burly stagehands carried me between them up a set of rickety, homemade, wooden stairs, my arms around their shoulders. Unable to put weight on my right foot, I had Chris Barber and Chad Eros, an accountant and board member, help me to the microphone and stay with me, on either side. I was feeling elated but mellow. The nerve block on my ankle had worn off, and I was popping tablets of an opioid medication called Dilaudid. I praised everybody for turning off the fake news, for coming to Ottawa, for coming together, and for unifying as one voice against government vaccine mandates.

"I've been asked a few times," I said, "'Why is it that you Canadians are so peaceful? Why don't Canadians ever fight? How come Canadians never argue?' And I say, 'Yes, we can be peaceful. We can be quiet and loving — right up to the point when we skate onto the ice to play hockey.' [cheers] And now we're on the ice. We're dressed for the game, our politicians have entered the rink, and we're not going to be pushed around." [loud cheers]

156

I was having fun, but even with a hockey joke I had to be careful. I gave a shoutout to Joël Lightbound for his scathing criticism of Trudeau, and to a Toronto Liberal MP, Nathaniel Erskine-Smith, for saying, "We don't have to vilify those who disagree with us." After about four minutes, I could feel myself already winding down.

"I apologize if I seem low-energy," I said. "I'm pumped full of painkillers after my surgery. We're overwhelmed by the love you've given us. We're going to remain peaceful. This is going to remain the biggest festival in Canada's history, an example to the world. Even people who criticize us are starting to realize that we're also here for them. Embrace them with your love. [cheers] Show peace and love and unity for your fellow citizens, even those who disagree with us." [cheers]

Afterward, the stagehands lowered me down the stairs again, and a small crowd gathered. People were thanking me and saying hello, and I slowly made my way on the crutches saying, "Hey guys, beep beep." Salman was walking ahead clearing the path.

"BJ, take this chair," a man said. He was pushing a wheelchair toward me, an old one with an ariel on the side flying a Canadian flag.

"No, no, I'll be okay — thanks," I said, but somebody else insisted.

"Take it," the person said. "Get somebody to bring it back."

"Thanks, but no, no."

To my right, I caught a glimpse of a man, late twenties, dressed in a red-and-blue snowsuit, furry hat over his head, and lying on the snow.

"Give him back his wheelchair," I said. "This is terrible. Don't let him lie there."

"We'll get him something to sit on," somebody said, and in a flash someone brought him a lawn chair.

"He wants you to use his wheelchair," another voice said.

"No, I'm not taking his mobility. He's done his part. He's come out. He's already given a lot."

We went back and forth. I felt terrible. All week I had been dealing with the egomaniacs at the ARC, and the man in the wheelchair was the opposite. He was humility itself. He was doing what B.C. organizer Colin Valentim talked about at the outset — take part in whatever way you can, big or small. "If you can't drive, be on the overpasses. Join from any part, from any location. Leave from any part, or any location. It doesn't really matter." The man was offering to help in a way that maybe nobody else in the crowd could. He wanted to lend me his wheelchair, his only means of getting around, a gesture in the true spirit of the Freedom Convoy. I couldn't make it over to him in the crowd, but he waved to me and I waved back, and Daniel and Salman wheeled me back to the Sheraton in his chair.

Chapter 26

Trudeau Invokes
the Emergencies Act

Brian Peckford chose not to get vaccinated after analyzing hospitalization admission numbers for COVID-19. To him, they looked relatively low, and he had concerns about potential vaccine side-effects. He declined the inoculation, and when the Trudeau government imposed a proof-of-vaccination policy for all airline travel, international and domestic, he found himself all but grounded on Vancouver Island, where he lives.

Peckford is the former premier of Newfoundland. He participated in the months of intense negotiations that led to the patriation from London in 1982 of the Canadian Constitution, with a new Charter of Rights and Freedoms. Justin Trudeau's father, Pierre Trudeau, was prime minister at the time. Of all the first ministers who helped hammer out the package, Peckford is the only participant still living. In late January, when the truck convoys started toward Ottawa, he sued the government in Federal Court over the travel vaccine mandate. He and five others argued that the mandate "effectively bans Canadians who have chosen not to receive an experimental medical treatment" from airplane travel. They rested their case on specific clauses of the Charter of Rights and Freedoms.

On the third weekend of the protest, Peckford flew to Ottawa by private plane to join the Freedom Convoy. He was our highest profile guest ever, a champion of the freedom movement, although the corporate media were doing their best to ignore him and his lawsuit. *To the Globe and Mail, the CBC, and pretty much* all other establishment news outlets, the one living former premier who helped draft the Charter, and who was now suing the government for violating his Charter rights, was not a story. On Monday, February 14, Day Seventeen, he and Tamara gave an open-invitation news conference in a room off the ARC Hotel lobby.

"This is a very, very strange moment in our history," Peckford began. He was dressed business-casual style, in a blue, button-down shirt, a patterned tie of mostly beiges and browns, and a finely knit lead-grey cardigan. He sat with his arms resting on the table in front of him, the fingers of both hands intertwined and wriggling like worms from a can. Originally, he had planned to speak about his constitutional challenge, but events were overtaking him. Word was going around that Trudeau was poised to invoke the Emergencies Act. It had never been used before. It had been passed thirty-four years earlier, in 1988, to replace the War Measures Act, which itself had been used only three times in Canadian history — during the two World Wars and the October Crisis of 1970.

"This is completely unnecessary to apply to the truckers," Peckford said of the Emergencies Act. It would be an "abomination response." The truckers were behaving "peacefully under legal and civil disobedience that has been part of our democracy."

By then, the Ambassador Bridge in Windsor had reopened. Local police working with the RCMP and OPP had arrested twenty-five to thirty people the day before and cleared the parked trucks. Everybody else had walked away. Traffic and trade were moving again in both directions. At the same time, negotiations had begun between Ottawa Mayor Watson and Freedom Convoy committee members to move the trucks off downtown Rideau Street.

"This is again a government overreach," Peckford said, tangling and untangling his fingers. "We don't do these kinds of things in Canada. We engage in dialogue, and it is my understanding that the Government of Canada has not reached out once to the truckers since they arrived in the capital city. I find that very hard to understand. How can you justify going to a measure like an Emergencies Act, where a lot of powers can be imposed upon the citizens, when you have not even yourself taken any action to engage first of all in dialogue? Let's forget the negotiations — just natural dialogue. To reach out to say, 'Can we sit down and have a talk? See where the major issues lie? And see if there is any common ground?'"

"Killing a fly with a sledgehammer," Peckford also said about using the act.

If the police move in, Tamara said, demonstrators will "hold the line."

"Hold the line," Peckford repeated.

When Pierre Trudeau announced his use of the War Measures Act in 1970, he addressed the nation on live television beginning with the words, "I am speaking to you at a moment of grave crisis, when violent and fanatical men are attempting to destroy the unity and the freedom of Canada."

By comparison, Justin Trudeau's declaration sounded trivial.

"I'm here to give you an update on the illegal blockades and tell you about our efforts to support Ukraine facing potential Russian invasion," he began in French. "But let's begin with the situation here in Canada, of course." Then he switched to English. "Illegal blockades have been disrupting the lives of too many Canadians," he said.

How many was too many, Trudeau didn't say. He stood at a podium with four senior ministers masked and spaced symmetrically behind him: Public Safety Minister Marco Mendicino, Finance Minister Chrystia Freeland, Attorney General David Lametti, and Emergency Preparedness Minister Bill Blair.

For the government to invoke the Emergencies Act, a certain threshold had to be met. The act defines a national emergency in two ways. One clause describes an "urgent and critical situation" that "seriously threatens the ability of the Government of Canada to preserve the sovereignty, security, and territorial integrity of Canada." That definition did not apply. The other clause identifies an "urgent and critical situation" that "seriously endangers the lives, health or safety of Canadians and is of such proportions or nature as to exceed the capacity or authority of a province to deal with it." That's the one Trudeau would use.

The emergency measures as applied would be "reasonable and proportionate to the threats," he said. He was short on specifics, preferring, as usual, to speak in generalities. He did,

162

however, offer two details. Under the measures, police could order tow-truck companies to tow away vehicles, and the RCMP would have the power to enforce municipal bylaws. While he acknowledged that the Ambassador Bridge had reopened, he said emergency powers were needed to make sure it stayed open. He described the use of the Emergencies Act as a "last resort," although he had tried nothing else. He would not call in the military, he also said.

Freeland spoke next, delivering the real news, the staggering news. She announced a weapon — a "tool," she called it — never before used against non-violent demonstrators in a Western democracy. She would use the Emergencies Act to order banks to freeze the personal and corporate accounts of protesters and their supporters. Their right to private property ownership would be suspended. Freeland would give the banks the names of those targeted. The banks would not need a court order to freeze the accounts, and they could never be prosecuted.

Freeland said she would also order the banks to report information on any customers involved in the protests to the RCMP or the Canadian Security Intelligence Service (CSIS). In addition, crowd-funding platforms such as GoFundMe and GiveSendGo, and those using Bitcoin or other digital currencies, would, under the emergency powers, be subject to Canada's anti-money laundering and terrorist-financing laws. All crowd-funding platforms would have to register with the Financial Transactions and Reports Analysis Centre, or FINTRAC. The government also planned to introduce new legislation, she said, to make the FINTRAC-related measures permanent.

"This is about following the money," Freeland said. "This is about stopping the financing of these illegal blockades."

Public Safety Minister Mendicino used his time at the podium to slander the protesters in the same vague terms the government and corporate media had been doing for more than two weeks. "We've seen intimidation, harassment, and expressions of hate," he said, "and at times the scenes on the streets of Wellington have seemed completely lawless."

All the ministers who spoke at the news conference repeated, over and over, the words "illegal" and "illegal blockades and occupations." At one point, asked about the Ottawa demonstration, Trudeau said, "It is no longer a lawful protest.... It is now an illegal occupation." He never explained how the demonstration went from "lawful" to "illegal." The answer seemed to be that the Emergencies Act gave him the power to declare it illegal. The Ottawa protest became illegal when he said so.

Ontario Premier Doug Ford welcomed the use of the emergency powers. "We need to do what it takes to restore law and order in our country," he said.

Others premiers pushed back.

"The Emergencies Act "must not apply in Quebec," Quebec Premier Francois Legault told Trudeau.

Manitoba Premier Heather Stefanson said emergency powers were "not necessary" to help her deal with the Emerson border blockade.

Saskatchewan Premier Scott Moe said the powers should only be used in provinces that request them, and he would not request them. "Police already have sufficient tools to enforce the law and clear the blockades, as they did over the weekend in Windsor," he said. "Therefore, Saskatchewan does not support the Trudeau government invoking the Emergencies Act."

Alberta Premier Jason Kenney, still dealing with the border blockade at Coutts, told Trudeau that emergency powers were not needed in his province, either. A few days later, Kenney said he would challenge the federal government's actions in court. The Emergencies Act is an "unnecessary" and "disproportionate" measure "that can violate civil liberties [and] invade provincial jurisdiction," he said. "It creates a very dangerous precedent for the future." Provincial police can deal with illegal blockades at Coutts and Windsor, he said. The rule of law must be applied, but people have the right to protest peacefully. Why, he asked rhetorically, would the federal government impose powers designed to interrupt terrorist financing to instead seize bank accounts and assets from people "arbitrarily, extra-judicially, without court orders, based on their opinions or who they've donated to?"

Two watchdog groups separately said they would sue the government in Federal Court. The Canadian Civil Liberties Association called the use of the Emergencies Act "unnecessary, unjustifiable, and unconstitutional." The Calgary-based Canadian Constitution Foundation took a similar position. Kenney said his government would also apply as an intervenor in both cases to support both plaintiffs.

Other critics weighed in. The world was taking notice.

"In less than a month, the prime minister has gone from dismissing the Freedom Convoy as a 'small fringe minority,' to invoking legislation that is designed for a foreign invasion or a civil war," wrote Carson Jerema, a columnist for Canada's *National Post*.

"For Justin Trudeau, emergency powers are too often a policy of first resort," wrote *Wall Street Journal* letters editor Elliot Kaufman.

The demonstration "ranks as a nuisance," not an emergency, and ought to be tolerated in the name of free speech, the *New York Times* said in an editorial, siding with the truckers against the Canadian government, as Tucker Carlson and Glenn Beck had. "We disagree with the protesters' cause, but they have a right to be noisy and even disruptive," the *Times* said. "Governments have a responsibility to prevent violence by protesters, but they must be willing to accept some degree of disruption by those seeking to be heard."

The Indian media couldn't resist poking fun. The news website PGurus published an editorial cartoon with two panels. The first showed Trudeau calling to an Indian farmer, "You have my support, go on, protest." The second showed Trudeau running in the opposite direction, chased by a truck marked "Karma."

"The government in India did not use any force to disperse the farmers," wrote Jagdish Batra in the *Times of India.* "It was giving liberty to a fault, but surely, it put Indian democracy at a much higher pedestal than the Canadian. However, Modi is not preaching to Canada in return!"

"Justin Trudeau is kind of the king of wokedom," said English broadcaster Piers Morgan. "He has been caught here in a trap of his own devices.... He would profess to be the most liberal guy you'd ever meet in your life, and yet he is behaving like a fascist."

Sky News Australia asked British intellectual and author Douglas Murray for his analysis. Speaking off the cuff, he put the case in a nutshell. "Any reasonable democratic leader should have been able to listen to the concerns of peaceful protesters," Murray said, "and try to, effectively, listen to their concerns, negotiate with them, pacify them where possible, give in where possible, and more, and from the very beginning Justin Trudeau totally eschewed that possibility. He called all of his critics all of the worst names imaginable. He slandered the truckers, he slandered the supporters of the truckers, and now he's moved to the next phase, not just sending in the police to very brutally end the protest in Ottawa, but using legislation, which I don't think any democratic government has previously used, against its citizens, ordering banks to stop the accounts of not only people involved in the protests but apparently [people who were] supporting the protests... This is absolutely totalitarian behaviour."

Chapter 27

The Police Crackdown Begins

Some of us thought the Emergencies Act might be another empty threat, like Chief Sloly's surge-and-contain plan or Mayor Watson's state-of-emergency ploy. Others thought Trudeau was champing at the bit, that he wanted nothing better than to crush the protest with a massive squad of riot cops. In any case, none of us called a meeting to discuss how to respond. Our decision had been made long before. We were going to "hold the line," as Tamara put it. We were going to stay put until the government addressed our demand to end the vaccine mandates. Some drivers would leave for their own reasons. Others would stay to see the protest through. Our attitude was, "If we remain peaceful, we'll be okay. If the government and the police get violent, they'll lose."

Almost as soon as Trudeau announced his special powers, he didn't seem to need them after all. The day before, police with regular powers reopened the Ambassador Bridge. Hours before he spoke, the protest at Coutts, Alberta, was also winding down. RCMP officers arrested thirteen people, seized a cache of firearms and ammunition, and charged four suspects with conspiracy to commit murder. The alleged offenders had arrived late and were not part of the main demonstration, police said, but the arrests cast a pall on the protest and everybody decided to leave. As the last rigs pulled away the next day, truckers stood together at attention to sing "O Canada," and shook hands with, and hugged, the RCMP officers.

"The infiltration of extreme elements... really changed things for us," organizer Marco Van Huigenbos said. "Our message has been one of peace, peaceful protest, and to keep that message strong we felt the best decision was to move out."

Over the next couple of days, more air seeped out of the balloon. In Surrey, B.C., the Pacific Highway crossing reopened after police, exercising routine enforcement practices, arrested a dozen protesters blocking the road. At Emerson, Manitoba, after several days of negotiations, demonstrators agreed to disperse, and the RCMP agreed to make no arrests, lay no charges, and tow away no vehicles.

In Ottawa, Police Chief Peter Sloly resigned under pressure, the scapegoat of political inaction. "I think he made the right decision," Mayor Watson said with his usual long face. Other changes quickly followed. Diane Deans was ousted as Police Services Board chair. The board's vice-chair resigned. A second board member resigned. A police officer from outside Ottawa accepted the job as interim chief, then withdrew, and the post went to Ottawa Deputy Chief Steve Bell.

By Thursday things were settling down. The national emergency, if there had ever been one, had all but dissipated.

Protests at a few provincial legislatures remained, but Trudeau had never made them an issue. With the barricades at the highways and bridges gone, all he had left to deal with were the semis parked in downtown Ottawa. Undaunted, Trudeau officially opened debate in the House of Commons on the Emergencies Act. Already, its powers were in effect, but both houses of Parliament had to vote in favour of its invocation or the act would be immediately suspended. Trudeau spoke almost as though the trucks were still blocking the borders. "For the good of all Canadians, the illegal blockades and occupations have to stop and the borders have to remain open," he told the House.

At a news conference afterward, Chrystia Freeland said she had given the RCMP a list of names of people and businesses whose accounts she wanted frozen. The RCMP had forwarded the names to financial institutions, and she had spoken directly with the heads of all the major banks and with the director of FINTRAC, the financial intelligence agency that monitors money laundering and terrorist financing. The government was compelling the banks to carry out its orders, she said, granting them immunity from prosecution. She would not say how many accounts she had ordered frozen or whether they included those of people who had simply donated to the crowdfunding platforms. In her language, Freeland was more precise than Trudeau, saying not that highways and bridges were blocked, but that the government was determined not to let protesters return to block them again, and was determined to clear the Ottawa demonstration. She also issued an ultimatum.

"If your truck is being used in these protests, your corporate accounts will be frozen," she said. "The insurance on your vehicle will be suspended. The consequences are real and they will bite. It is time for you to go home. And let me also be clear that we will have zero tolerance for the establishments of new blockades or occupations. We now have the tools to follow the money. We can see what is happening and what is being planned in real time, and we are absolutely determined that this must end, now and for good."

For three weeks, convoy leaders had been telling the government it could easily end the protests by rescinding the mandates. Now Freeland reworked the sentence and threw it back at us. "There is a really easy way to avoid being affected by these measures," she said. "Go home, go back to work."

That evening, separately, police arrested Chris Barber and Tamara Lich on the street, cuffing their hands behind their back and taking them to jail. Barber was charged with counselling to commit mischief, counselling to disobey a court order, and counselling to obstruct police. Lich was charged with counselling mischief and additionally charged later with mischief, obstructing police, counselling to obstruct police, intimidation, and counselling intimidation.

The next day, Barber was granted bail and he returned to Saskatchewan. Lich got snagged in the legal system. The bail judge reserved her decision to the following week, then denied Lich bail, keeping her incarcerated. Lich appealed and after two and a half weeks won her release on strict conditions. In June, a court granted her permission to attend a Toronto banquet where the Justice Centre for Constitutional Freedoms was to present her with the George Jonas Freedom Award. Afterward, a video of less than three seconds surfaced showing Freedom Convoy truck captain Tom Marazzo congratulating her at the banquet, along with a snapshot of Lich and Marazzo standing next to each other in a group. On June 28, on a Canada-wide warrant, an Ottawa police detective arrested Lich in her home town of Medicine Hat for breach of bail conditions, i.e. standing next to Marazzo. The detective flew her to Ottawa, and on July 8 a judge revoked Lich's bail, committing her to jail until trial. Lich appealed a second time and on August 3 again won her release after a total of forty-nine days behind bars. Lich supporters deemed her a "political prisoner." By comparison, a man charged with driving into a crowd of demonstrators at a Freedom Convoy support rally in Winnipeg in February, injuring four people and fleeing the scene, was granted bail right away.

On Friday, Day Twenty-One, four days after Trudeau invoked his emergency powers, the most dramatic stage of the crackdown began. Police expanded their "Red Zone." They cordoned off a three-square-kilometre downtown area bounded by Wellington Street to the north, the Queensway expressway to the south, Bronson Avenue to the west, and the Rideau Canal to the east. At its perimeter, officers created 100 checkpoints to control access. Only people who could prove they lived, worked, or otherwise had a lawful reason to be in the area could enter. Wanting to join the protest was not a lawful reason, police said. Journalists not already in the zone were also prohibited from entering. At the end of the afternoon, they could attend a news conference outside the Red Zone.

Former RCMP sniper Daniel Bulford approached a police line near the Château Laurier and turned himself in. "The news says I'm to be arrested, is that true?" he said and police cuffed him. Pat King, ever the drama queen, livestreamed police knocking on his car door and telling him he was under arrest for counselling mischief, counselling to obstruct police, and counselling to disobey a court order. "Please step out of your vehicle, sir," an officer said.

"I'd like to get my lawyer on the phone right away," King said into the camera, staying put for the moment, putting off the inevitable.

A sleet-like rain turned to snow. In front of the Senate Building, the former central railway station, lines of police took up formation. All wore helmets and visors. All wore black uniforms with no names or badge numbers. In the first row, officers walking shoulder-to-shoulder held riot shields and hardwood batons. They advanced slowly, painstakingly, systematically. They took two or three steps toward the crowd, stopped for several minutes, took another two or three steps, and stopped again. In a second line behind them, officers kept pace carrying assault rifles and pepper-spray launchers. The officers left gaps between them, allowing those in a third line to quickly advance to attack and arrest anybody not moving back with the rest of the crowd. Over the weekend, nearly 200 arrests would be made.

At one point, suddenly, the Toronto Mounted Police Unit appeared. Video cameras tracked them from every angle, including above from a drone. The giant horses threaded a line between the police and the crowd, forcing the crowd back and trampling two protesters. One, a man, was never identified. Police swarmed him and have refused to release any information about him or his condition. The other was Candice Sero, a forty-nine-year-old woman with a walker, from the Tyendinaga Mohawk reserve near Belleville. Moments before the horse struck her, she was chanting, "Peace, love, happiness." Two months later, the police Special Investigations Unit said she sustained no injury other than a strained shoulder. Sero, on the other hand, reported on Facebook that she was taken to hospital, was diagnosed with a fractured clavicle, and had "a great big hoof print" on her hip.

Asked for further details, her lawyer said Sero had no further comment.

Some police officers were caught laughing about the event.

"Just watched that horse video — that is awesome," an officer identified only as Marca posted to an RCMP chat room on WhatsApp. "We should practice that manoeuvre."

"Time for the protesters to hear our jackboots on the ground," wrote Constable Andrew Nixon.

When the comments surfaced publicly, the RCMP issued a press release saying the force was investigating. "This material," a spokesperson said, "is not representative of those who have committed themselves to serving Canadians with integrity and professionalism."

Chapter 28

Dave Live from the Shed

Saturday was clean-up day. The riot squads had seized control of most of downtown. Many of the truckers had pulled out. Only a few dozen stalwarts on Wellington Street and adjacent blocks were left for the police to deal with. In some ways, the day was shaping up as an anti-climax, with the TV-equipment vans gone and the Parliamentary reporters' gallery reduced to a skeleton, weekend crew. The citizen journalists, however, remained active, walking the streets streaming their smartphone video to the internet. After the mass police and horse operations of the day before, international interest remained high, and the independent reporters assigned themselves to broadcast, unfiltered, what was about to unfold.

Perhaps nobody played a more central role in recording the final act in the Freedom Convoy than David Paisley, now better known as "Dave Live from the Shed." In many ways, he was typical of the people who came to Ottawa to support the truckers, and in many ways his story is that of the grassroots nature of the movement.

Paisley holds a technician's job in the Waterloo district of southwestern Ontario. He likes to keep details vague because of anti-convoy internet trolls, of which there remain many. In late January 2022, online, he came across videos of the western convoys, along with posts saying Ontario trucks would soon be coming through. He didn't have much information, but one afternoon he finished work early and drove to an interchange south of Guelph, where Highway 6 passes over Highway 401.

It was a cold afternoon, minus twenty and blowing. At the bridge, he expected he might see a few other people, but nearly two hundred, including children, were already waiting. Somebody handed him a Canadian flag. Somebody else gave him a cup of hot chocolate. Eventually, trucks started passing, not in a solid line like the western convoys, but in bunches. One truck stood out for him, a flatbed carrying a plywood fishing shed.

Paisley is a naturally social person. He had negotiated the pandemic as best he could, doing his part, but had grown annoyed at what he saw as government overreach. Issuing health guidelines was one thing but ordering businesses to close was another. He had never been to a protest, but when he saw the trucks he was ready.

"Like a lot of folks, I sat and complained to my friends, and that was about it," he says in retrospect, "until I joined the people waiting for the convoy. It was like a spiritual experience for me. I knew I had to get to Ottawa. I thought, 'This needs to happen. The time is now.'"

Right away, he texted friends. Some were already thinking about going, too, and the next day, Friday, they loaded themselves into a crew cab pickup truck, with two rows of seats, drove to Kingston, and from there joined a convoy into the nation's capital. "It was crazy," he says.

For the first weekend, Paisley and his friends shared a hotel room, but almost immediately he knew he had to stay longer. The packed streets, the flags, the laughter, the joyful atmosphere — "There was something powerful happening and I wanted to be part of it," he says. He called his boss and got time off. A businessman friend who couldn't be there paid his hotel bill for the next week, and Paisley set about making himself useful.

"Everybody wanted to get involved and I focused on Wellington Street," he says. "That's where everybody was congregating and taking pictures, and the Parliament Buildings were right there. A bunch of trucks with the Peace Tower as the backdrop is dramatic. That can't be ignored. I felt if we could keep Wellington Street, we could keep this thing going for as long as we needed."

The regional team structure that had helped get the convoys to Ottawa had dissolved, and Paisley helped build a street-level organization. He started talking to drivers. He climbed into trucks and introduced himself and tried to figure out what was going on. One of his first encounters was with Jason "Jay" VanderWier, the trucker who had mounted a fishing shed on his flatbed as a place to sleep during the protest. He was from Smithville, in the Niagara Region, and, like most of the truckers parked on Wellington, he hadn't officially registered with a convoy. He had come on his own and parked next to what became the stage truck, at the west side of the Wellington and Metcalfe intersection — the central square, the heart of the protest.

Paisley and VanderWier hit it off. Together, they decided to create a local community. Several subgroups were forming.

Truckers from Quebec lined the block immediately east of Metcalfe, and truckers from Alberta and Saskatchewan were parked still farther east near the Château Laurier. Paisley and VanderWier circulated among the Ontario drivers west of the square and held meetings in the shed about food, fuel, and other needs.

Food distribution channels formed quickly. Donations were plentiful and police never tried to confiscate them. "We had wood-fired pizza, a burger tent, pastas, soups — I never had to think about eating," Paisley says. He turned his attention to fuel-supply lines. He saw people carrying jerry cans and asked to help. He hitched a ride to the Coventry staging depot to learn about the bigger picture. He kept adding to his contact list and helped streamline a fuel distribution system to the downtown, and, as their street organization became better defined, he and VanderWier shared the role of Wellington "block captain," attending daily morning meetings at the ARC Hotel.

Paisley kept extending his stay. He booked a hotel for a second week, then a third, letting truckers use his room during the day to shower, or take a break from their rig. VanderWier made additions to the shed. He built a pair of latrines at the back and designed an observation platform. The shed roof sloped on both sides. With smuggled lumber, a couple of carpenters built a rooftop platform, complete with a railing on all four sides and a stairway to the top. When demonstrators kept climbing the steps to take pictures, the carpenters added a door to control access. Paisley and VanderWier allowed mainly news reporters, camera operators, and vloggers on the platform in exchange for their contact information.

As the protest entered its third week, Paisley attached a camera to the platform's top railing and wired it to a laptop, like a security system. If the police moved in, the camera would track their movements and he would have a record. The system quickly evolved. Paisley had seen citizen journalists walking the streets with smartphones streaming the protest live. He had even met some of the livestreamers — Zot, Ottawalks, UOttawaScotty, and drone specialist Tanner O'Crane of TireRoastersGarage, who had travelled with the convoy from Alberta.

Paisley liked what they were doing. From YouTube tutorials, he taught himself how to convert his camera into a webcam that could simultaneously record to his laptop and broadcast live to the internet. "Live from the Shed" was born. A young graphic designer from North Bay, Tikvah Tignanelli, designed a logo for him, somebody else found a supportive printing company, and by the end of the day Paisley had red-and-white banners with a "Live from the Shed" logo hanging from the platform railings.

He started streaming video of Wellington Street, looking west. For a wider view, he bought a 360-degree camera, then a second camera, which he pointed east. Throughout the protest, Henry's camera store and Canada Computers did a booming business as convoy supporters upgraded their equipment. When internet access proved spotty, he posted a sign on the shed to say, "Elon Musk, We Need Starlink." It was a joke, but within the hour somebody offered to drive home a couple of hours away in Quebec and return with his Starlink disc, giving Paisley access to Musk's broadband satellite service. To broadcast live on YouTube, he also needed 1,000 subscribers minimum, and when Montreal-based vlogger Viva Frei interviewed him about his project, Paisley's audience numbers exploded. "I was blown away by how much interest there was," he says. "Very quickly, thousands of people at a time were watching this thing."

Trudeau invoked the Emergencies Act. Tensions escalated. Police arrived en masse into the city and made the first arrests — Chris and Tamara. Late the same night, sitting by himself in the shed, bored, watching the lines of comments scroll up the page as he broadcast the scenes of Wellington Street on a split screen, Paisley decided to reply to messages for the first time. When he answered the first question, he recalls, "the chat went crazy. People were desperate for information."

The next day was Friday, February 18, the day the police and horses cleared the crowd to within one block east of the shed truck. Paisley knew all of Wellington would be next. Maybe the police would come that night. He gave his spare hotel key to VanderWier and elected to stay to broadcast and record events. By late evening nothing had happened. The police must be waiting for morning, he thought, but he decided to stay up anyway. Sometime after midnight, alone and bored again, he turned on a microphone he had just bought and spoke live to his audience for the first time.

"If you just listened to the mainstream media you might think there's just a handful of crazy people and a few trucks, but the real story is much more amazing," he told listeners. "This is an incredible grassroots movement of people of all ages and all walks of life."

He talked about who he was and how he got involved. Livestreaming was new to him, he said. He only started a few days ago. In the comments, listeners asked him to turn on the donation function and to stream simultaneously to Rumble. He said he didn't know where the donation function was, and he had tried to stream to Rumble but couldn't get it to work. He was new at this, he said, learning on the fly.

Paisley talked for five hours, right through the night. He answered questions about the arrests and the general mood among the truckers. In the wee hours, the broadcast became more intimate. He was like Christian Slater in the 1990 film *Pump up the Volume*, a lonely high school student on his pirate-radio station connecting emotionally with other lonely high school students needing to hear an understanding and compassionate voice. Paisley shared what he had been going through, and at one point started tenderly reading messages on the children's drawings that VanderWier had plastered on the shed walls. "Thank you, truckers." "You are my hero." "You will give us our freedom back." He talked until the first light returned to the sky, when truckers with shovels could be seen on the webcam scraping freshly fallen snow from the street.

A couple of hours later, riot police and special tactical units moved in. Paisley continued his live video feed and revived his commentary, later archived on YouTube as "The Last Stand of the Shed."

"You can hear the noises of people getting shoved around outside," he says on the feed, cameras showing the scene.

Riot police surround a man on the ground. One officer takes four powerful lunges at him, connecting each time with a right knee.

"That's terrible," Paisley says.

People are shouting. The next sounds are of boots above on the shed platform. Out of camera range, tactical officers in dun-coloured uniforms are arresting a bearded demonstrator named "Peaceman," who had climbed to the platform to flash peace signs with his fingers. A minute later, also out of camera range, the shed door opens. Paisley sees the muzzle of a gun pointed at his chest.

"Get on the ground," the tactical officer snaps.

"Yes, sir."

"Right now. Stay still."

The officer cuffs Paisley behind his back with a zip tie and leads him outside. He is made to stand by a car. He is in view of one of his cameras now. One officer hands him off to another, and then another. Eventually he is told he will not be charged, but he is made to get into a van to be dropped outside the Red Zone, he's not sure where, but half an hour out of downtown. With the help of the Capital City Bikers' Church, he returns downtown, using his hotel key card to get past police roadblocks, but the story doesn't end there.

New York Times reporter Sarah Maslin Nir, who had been following developments, called Paisley from New York, and as he was describing the morning's events, she stopped him. The police arrested him at gunpoint? Was he sure? Could he corroborate it? Did he know anybody else who had a gun pointed at them?

Paisley asked around. He was still at the Bikers' Church and found somebody with a similar story. He also contacted a vlogger named Church of BuBBles, who said he had video of the officer entering the shed with his gun raised and pointed. Another vlogger had footage of tactical police entering a nearby camper van with guns raised. The *Times* reporter had her story. She wrote it with a colleague under the headline, "Ottawa Protesters Cleared from Parliament Encampment." In part, her second and third paragraphs read this way:

"Starting about 10 a.m., police advanced on trucks that had been parked on Wellington Street, the thoroughfare in front of the Parliament building, drawing guns on some vehicles and banging on doors as they searched for any people inside… One demonstrator, David Paisley, a HVAC technician who has spent the protest broadcasting updates from a fishing shack on the back of a flatbed truck known as "the shed," described the moment an officer entered the vehicle to arrest him. 'He had a big military rifle, he pointed right at my chest, he yelled at me to get down, on the ground,' said Paisley... who captured the moment of his arrest on a recorded livestream. 'It was like a movie scene.'"

On Twitter, the *New York Times* posted the story. "Breaking News," the subject line read. "The police arrested demonstrators at gunpoint near the Parliament building in Ottawa..."

If anybody needed more evidence that the CBC, the *Globe and Mail*, and rest of the Canadian corporate media were spreading fake news about the Freedom Convoy — and censoring legitimate news — they got it that day. On Twitter, the backlash to the *Times* story was swift and profuse. Leading members of the Canadian media elite refused to believe that Canadian police would point a gun at a Freedom Convoy demonstrator, and blamed the messenger.

"Hey New York Times: If you don't want to send reporters to the scene then all you have to do is watch Canadian TV," *As It Happens* host Carol Off, in Toronto, said without apparent irony. "Try a bit harder to get this story right."

"Omg NYT: is this how you do reporting on 'foreign' stories?" asked long-time CBC Radio host Piya Chattopadhyay. "You are better than this. So do better."

"This is false and incredibly dangerous rhetoric that will be used by those with no interest in facts," wrote Ginella Massa, host of *Canada Tonight with Ginella Massa* on the CBC cable news network.

"That [New York Times] tweet is reprehensibly inaccurate," said Dr. Brian Goldman, a Toronto physician with a national CBC radio show.

"This requires a correction," wrote senior *Globe and Mail* Ottawa reporter and columnist John Ibbitson. "Unless weapons were drawn and pointed at protesters then this is both factually incorrect and dangerous to assert."

"Guns were not drawn," said the ubiquitous Justin Ling, Freedom Convoy authority for the CBC, the *Toronto Star*, and *Maclean's* magazine. "This is wrong."

"Is the @nytimes drunk? Where are the guns?" said Stephanie Carvin, a former federal government national-security issues analyst, a Carleton University professor, and a sometime CBC, CNN, and *Globe and Mail* guest and contributor. "Ottawa police have not covered themselves in glory but what they are doing is not 'at gunpoint.'"

"Y'all, just call me," said Fatima Syed, vice-president of the Canadian Association of Journalists, using mock American vernacular. "I'll write the right, accurate story for you because this is embarrassing and wrong."

At independent Rebel News, Ezra Levant compiled the Twitter reaction, along with photos and video of police with guns raised and pointed at four separate vehicles, not including the shed. One of the photos shows a group of heavily-armed tactical police, with at least three officers clearly pointing raised guns at a mobile home and into the open back door.

The *New York Times* stood by its story. The paper might be a corporate news organization, but it does not take money from the Trudeau government or tailor its coverage to the wishes of the Prime Minister's Office.

The riot police and tactical units kept going. If drivers refused to unlock their doors, police smashed their windows. If drivers continued to passively resist, the police dragged them into the snow and smacked them with rifle butts. Then police towed away the trucks.

Chapter 29

This was Bitcoin's Moment

He was an Ottawa physiotherapist who specialized in feet. In 2015, he had a patient who liked to talk about Bitcoin, the decentralized, digital currency that first came into use in 2009. To chat intelligently with his patient, the physiotherapist started to learn about Bitcoin and bought an entire digital coin for $140. At the same time, he continued to grow his business. He developed an online health network focused on feet and began travelling the world giving workshops. In the two years preceding the COVID-19 pandemic, he conducted seventy events in eleven countries.

The company was building a cash reserve for new projects, but because the government kept printing money the fund's purchasing power was depreciating. Between January 2020 and January 2021, the physiotherapist calculated that it "just melted 18.5 per cent in one year," which he also viewed as a devaluation of his own stored life energy. At the end of 2021, he stepped down as head of the company to commit more time to Bitcoin. Over the long term, it seemed obvious to him that Bitcoin would hold its value better than "fiat money" — currency issued and controlled by the government and centralized banks. As a way to educate himself further, he hosted a podcast called *Bitcoin Stoa* "to have good conversations with really smart people," he says. One month later the Freedom Convoy arrived in Ottawa.

Online, the physiotherapist identifies himself to other Bitcoiners as "Caribou." Pseudonyms are a Bitcoin tradition. Its inventor, or inventors, identify themselves as Satoshi Nakamoto, and the smallest Bitcoin unit is the "satoshi," or "sat," worth one hundred-millionth of one coin. Caribou lived a forty-minute walk from Wellington Street. On the opening Friday, he strolled through the crowd holding a placard above his head saying, "Opt Out Buy Bitcoin," with a red maple leaf at the bottom. He was wearing a heavy parka, huge mitts, reflective sunglasses, a toque sporting the Bitcoin logo, and a bright smile. Somebody took a picture and posted it to Twitter.

In Oakville, outside Toronto, former hedge-fund manager and Bitcoin strategist Greg Foss saw the tweet and recognized Caribou despite the heavy clothing. They had never met but had been on a podcast together.

"I reached out to Nick," Foss recalls. "I said, 'We've got to start a Bitcoin wallet to raise money for these guys, because I know [the protest] resonates with Bitcoiners.'"

"Hey, can you help?" Caribou replied. "You've got a big [social media] following."

"Yes," Foss said. With so much money flowing into the GoFundMe account, making the government look bad, both thought the government would try to shut it down.

Throughout the first weekend Caribou talked to truckers. "I did two shifts a day," he says. "I went out in the morning, came home, recovered, wrote some notes, then I did an afternoon shift. I would ask, 'How can I help? What do you need?' and they would say, 'We need coffee. We need toilets. I would love to spend a night in a hotel room.' I thought, 'All right, I'll raise some Bitcoin. Some people know how to bake cookies. Some people know how to get fuel. This is something I can do for the people sacrificing so much for Canadians, even if most Canadians have no idea what's truly happening.'"

"Working on a #Bitcoin donation strategy to support the Freedom Convoy," he posted to Twitter. "Good chance to show the world how bitcoin fixes financial censorship."

Sometimes during his visits to the rigs, Caribou offered drivers an "orange pill," slang for information about Bitcoin. The term is often used as a verb. He was "orange pilling" the drivers, telling them about monetary freedom from governments and banks — monetary sovereignty. On the Sunday of the first weekend, in a thirty-minute session, he showed a trucker from Saskatoon named Jason how to download a digital wallet onto his phone. Caribou transferred 50,021 "sats" to him. At the time, the amount was worth $28 Canadian, a small donation, but it was a start.

By Monday, after the first weekend, some Bitcoiners were starting to question online where the donations were going. Where there is fundraising there is suspicion. To give the campaign the stamp of integrity, Foss recruited Jeff Booth, the éminence grise of the Canadian Bitcoin community. He is also a Vancouver-area technology entrepreneur and author of an economics treatise called *The Price of Tomorrow: Why Deflation is the Key to an Abundant Future*. Booth said he would endorse the Bitcoin fundraiser to support people engaged in non-violent protest. "I told

Greg [Foss] I think democracy requires freedom of speech," he recalls. "I would even support, on principle, [a crowdfunding campaign for] an issue I disagreed with."

For technical support, Foss and Booth further enlisted a Calgary YouTuber and orange-piller who calls himself BTC Sessions, meaning "Bitcoin Sessions." He opened an account with Tallycoin, a Bitcoin crowdfunding platform that accepts payments through the Lightning Network, which makes transfers almost instant, like a credit-card transfer service.

Sessions linked the Tallycoin campaign to a Twitter account he created called #HonkHonkHodl. "HonkHonk" was a reference to the trucks in Ottawa. "Hodl" was a Bitcoin in-joke. During a volatile phase for the currency, a Bitcoiner advised people not to sell their Bitcoin but to "hodl" it, mistyping "hold." At the Freedom Convoy, the typo took on an additional role. When Tamara Lich started using the term "hold the line," Bitcoiners endorsed the stand with "hodl the line."

One week into the demonstration, Caribou got in touch with me. He had seen the #Bitcoin hashtag on my Twitter page and knew I must be a Bitcoiner. Like him, I also started in 2015. On the second Saturday of the demonstration, bundled in snow boots and parkas, he and a dozen other Bitcoiners spilled into my media suite seeking to involve the convoy leadership in the Tallycoin campaign.

This was Bitcoin's moment, we told each other. For years, Bitcoiners had spoken hypothetically about digital currency protecting people against tyrannical governments, and from banks cutting people off from their money. Now it was happening. The day before, under police and political pressure, GoFundMe cancelled our account, and the TD Bank continued to freeze the first $1 million. In response, Tallycoin donations were surging past the $300,000 mark.

"This is a chance for Bitcoin to prove itself," Caribou told the group. "We can't screw this up. We have to really put our brains together and make sure this is done right because this is Bitcoin on a world stage."

A few days later, Caribou returned to the Sheraton to speak at one of our news conferences. It's hard to get reporters to see Bitcoin as a story if they know nothing about it, but he did his best. "It's a global financial network that is uncensorable, permissionless, and when you do it properly it is unconfiscateable," he said. "To show the power of this technology, I want to share some of the messages from our donors." Tiny donations were arriving from all parts of the world — Nepal, Hong Kong, Australia, Scandinavia, India, several European countries, South America, and Africa, maybe fifty different countries. Caribou read a few of the notes.

"Sipping a coffee in Hong Kong making my daily donation, who will join me?" (CAD$1.27)

"The sat-streaming shall continue until the freedom improves." (105 sats, 5 cents).

"Just watched Ottawa police bullying a peaceful citizen. Hope this helps with the lawsuit." ($3.80)

"Go truckers. Thanks for fighting for my freedoms." (200 sats, 11 cents)

"That last one was from a doctor in Nigeria," Caribou said. "Giving 200 sats was his vote for freedom. He wanted to support non-violent demonstrators fighting to make their voices heard."

Caribou then floated a new idea. Maybe he was just thinking out loud. "We have the option to create something like a Bitcoin endowment for truckers," he told reporters. A fund could be created that would send sats to every Freedom Convoy trucker every month for years, until the endowment is liquidated. "It becomes a powerful way to show these truckers the appreciation for the sacrifices they've made and to really be able to harness the power of Bitcoin."

Four days later, Caribou went on YouTube with an update. The fund had reached its goal: 21 Bitcoin, worth more than CAN$1 million at the time. He and BTC Sessions had closed the fund to further contributions in order to focus on distribution. Caribou said nothing more about an endowment. Instead, he talked about the challenge of getting the busy convoy board members to a meeting. He also ran through how he would transfer the donations to recipients, using a protocol that Sessions had developed. A single digital wallet would be created to hold the funds, he said. Multiple signatures would be required for withdrawals. Five people — five keyholders — would hold signing authority, and each transfer would require three signatures. The five keyholders would be Caribou, Foss, Booth, me, and one other person. Sitting at his desktop microphone in his apartment, Caribou elaborated.

"The ideal multi-sig, from a security and privacy perspective, would be something like a cold card with a Specter desktop wallet, but the reality on the ground here is that that's a big ask for Newbies," he said. "That's why we're going with Nunchuk. It's our best option. It's a very user friendly interface and we have a great support team on the technical side that will walk through the directors of the non-profit to make sure they get set up properly."

The pieces were falling into place. Caribou was finding his way. Nobody had any experience trying to get Bitcoin to members of a mass political demonstration while the government and the banks were actively blocking financial aid. Just as he was making progress, however, everything changed. Trudeau invoked the Emergencies Act. Freeland said the Bitcoin fundraiser would be subject to federal money-laundering and terrorist-financing laws, apparently meaning that it would now be against the law. Foss, Booth, and the fifth keyholder withdrew. They disagreed with the law, they said, but they would obey it. That left Caribou and me, and because the convoy board never came around to adopting the Bitcoin fundraiser, I also had to withdraw. That left only Caribou. He found a second keyholder and resolved to go ahead.

Then another hitch arose. A prominent Bitcoiner in the United States calling himself JW Weatherman came across the video with the endowment idea. Outraged, he posted a questionnaire. "When you donated to #HonkHonkHodl did you expect them to do something like: immediately distribute an equal amount of bitcoin to every trucker; or setup an organization that might not fully pay it out for many years?" When more than half the respondents said they expected immediate payouts, Weatherman threatened to sue the organizers. "You'll find out how much I donated because I will double it in legal fees if you don't back down from keeping the bitcoin for years," he said. Specifically, he said he would sue Foss and Sessions "if the bitcoin isn't distributed to truckers before the protest is over."

Everything was happening fast. Weatherman was lagging behind. By the time he made his threat, Foss and Sessions were already out of the picture. Caribou knew he would be the next target, but he got an idea.

Chapter 30

Bitcoin Proves its Power

JW Weatherman is a leading Bitcoin security expert. Partly, he is known for a seminal document called "Bitcoin Threat Model: A Security Review of the Bitcoin Cryptocurrency," published on the open-source software development platform GitHub. For years, he has been creating free educational content for people wanting to learn about Bitcoin.

"I reached out to him," Caribou says. "I told him, 'Regardless of what I do, you're going to be my harshest critic. Could you help me? You have the deepest technical understanding of almost anybody. Why don't you tell me how you would do it?' And he said, 'All right, I kind of got myself into this.'"

Right away, Weatherman went to work. He hosted online meetings with other specialists to design a methodology for distributing Bitcoin to truckers. In response, somebody wrote an initial script. In a Twitter Space audio forum, Weatherman then led dozens of participants in subjecting the script to scrutiny. They offered suggestions and made changes. At the same time, at Weatherman's prompting, Caribou consulted lawyer friends, who assured him he was within his legal rights to allocate the funds to the truckers.

It was now Wednesday, February 16. The Emergencies Act was into its third day. Caribou spent two and a half hours loading software he would need into his laptop, and the laptop crashed. He went out and bought a new one. He also bought an ink cartridge and printing paper. "There were a million obstacles," he says. Eventually, with Weatherman's guidance, he loaded the software into the new laptop. He ran a script to create 100 digital wallets, got the second keyholder's signature, loaded Bitcoin into the wallets, and printed 100 copies of a five-page document with a private key and instructions on how to access and ultimately spend the Bitcoin. He then stuffed the documents into brown, legal-size envelopes.

By eight o'clock that night he was ready. Carrying forty envelopes worth $320,000 in his backpack, he left for Wellington Street, and for the next four hours, until midnight, he handed the envelopes to drivers in their rigs. A friend recorded each delivery. Some of the drivers Caribou knew from earlier visits. Others he knew only by sight or not at all, and he had to explain what he was doing.

"I had a little speech written out," he says. "I had to knock on the window, introduce myself, explain what the envelope was, give it to them, thank them, and move on. I had to literally build enough trust in three or four minutes for them not to take the envelope and throw it away. The truckers were nervous. Police had been lying to them. It would have been easy for them to think I was just trying to rip them off."

196

The next day was Thursday, February 17. Tensions were building. Tamara and Chris would be arrested that day. Freeland would tell a news conference that afternoon, "We now have the tools to follow the money." All morning, Caribou went truck to truck delivering envelopes of paper codes and instructions. He went home for lunch, returned in the afternoon, went home for a nap, and returned in the evening.

During his final shift, he was feeling anxious. Fortunately, snow started to fall, obscuring his movements, and for extra cover he crumpled waste paper into a garbage bag and mixed the Bitcoin envelopes with the paper. Volunteers were going truck to truck asking drivers if they had any garbage to throw out, and Caribou pretended he was one of them, except he was also carrying $400,000 in digital currency. "I was just a dude walking around with a garbage bag," he says. "I had a big smile on my face the whole time."

A video posted to Twitter that day captures one encounter. A trucker is giving an interview in his rig to a citizen journalist. "Every few days," the trucker is saying, "there's some BS about — hey, man."

Caribou suddenly appears at the open driver-side window. "I'm going to give this to you," he says, handing the trucker a brown envelope decorated with sparkly stickers. "Remember how I came and got you some sats?"

"Yep, yep."

"There's eight grand in Bitcoin in there," Caribou says.

"In here?"

"In there. As soon as the banks shut down, we got some big donors that were like, 'We need to get Bitcoin to these truckers.'"

"You're kidding."

"Open it up. There's instructions…. It's going to tell you to download BlueWallet, which is what the recovery code is for. It will be a different wallet than the first one I showed you."

"Right."

"Boot it up, it's yours."

"That's insane, man."

"Thanks for your service."

"That's ridiculous."

"No, Dude, you came all the way here to save our country — *that's* ridiculous. Thank you from the Bitcoin community. I'll see you around."

"Thanks, man."

Caribou and the driver shake hands, and as Caribou leaves the driver turns again to the camera.

"You guys caught it, good timing," he says. "I just met that guy a couple, I don't know, a week ago," he says. "He had a Bitcoin toque on and I said, 'What's up with that?' He said, 'Actually, if you don't mind — ' So I let him sit in the truck, and we downloaded his wallet or whatever, and he said there's some massive freedom loving people out there… and apparently there's eight grand of Bitcoin in here…. That's definitely one of the craziest things that's happened in the last two weeks."

That night, Caribou returned home exhausted. In twenty-four hours, he had distributed the equivalent of CAN$800,000 in $8,000 packages to "90-ish" truckers, he says. For the last few, he doubled the donation, because by then most drivers had gone to bed and weren't answering a knock on the window.

"Unstoppable freedom money to support Canadians claiming their freedom," he posted to Twitter. "Protocol created by the Bitcoin community, led by #JWWeatherman. Thanks to everyone who gave their sats and their input over DMs."

"I've done some hard things in my life," Caribou says in retrospect, "but this was probably the hardest. The most challenging and the most fulfilling. The thanks I got, the hugs I got, just the honour of being able to hand out money that was raised by the global Bitcoin community was very powerful."

A few days later, twelve police officers representing the RCMP, OPP, and the Ottawa Police Service pushed themselves into Caribou's small apartment with a warrant to seize the leftover Bitcoin donations, worth nearly $300,000. A software glitch had prevented Caribou from moving some Bitcoin from an earlier multi-sig wallet. By the time he solved the problem, he had been served a court order not to move the funds. The police warrant alleged "possession of property obtained by crime, money laundering, and mischief to property," he says, but the police did not charge him with a crime, and he was not under arrest. Instead, police escorted him to an unmarked vehicle and demanded that he turn over the recovery codes, or "seed phrases," to the remaining Bitcoin, which he did. The funds have since been moved into an escrow account pending the outcome of Zexi Li's class-action lawsuit.

At the end of February, the deputy director of intelligence at FINTRAC, the money-laundering and terrorism-financing analysis unit, testified that the Freedom Convoy crowdfunding campaigns posed no security threat to Canada. Without addressing Freeland's actions directly, he essentially contradicted her rationale. His statement also meant that the police warrant used to raid Caribou's apartment and seize funds was unfounded.

"I think that there were people around the world who were fed up with COVID, who were upset and saw the demonstrations against COVID [mandates], and I believe that they just wanted to support the cause," Barry MacKillop told the House of Commons finance committee. "It was… their own money, so it wasn't money that funded terrorism, or was in any way money laundering."

Bitcoin was the only crowdfunded currency to reach the truckers — $800,000 worth. Through GoFundMe the convoy raised $10.1 million. Most was returned to donors. The other $1 million that TD Bank refused to release went into escrow pending the outcome of the class-action lawsuit. Of the nearly $10 million raised through GiveSendGo, much was returned to donors and much went into escrow. Depending on the lawsuit's outcome, the escrow account could go either to truckers or to downtown Ottawa residents, but already the fund is being siphoned off by lawyers engaged in court proceedings.

How much Bitcoin police might have tracked after Caribou distributed it to the truckers is not publicly known. Bitcoin transactions are pseudonymous but not anonymous. They are recorded on a public ledger, subject to police scrutiny. In March, without commenting directly on the Freedom Convoy, the RCMP issued a statement to the CBC that police have the capability to seize and recover digital currency assets and that in the past the Crown has successfully prosecuted crypto criminals. On the other hand, said a lawyer quoted in the story, Bitcoin can be transferred from wallet to wallet indefinitely to obscure the original source, making recovery by government and police authorities difficult. Months after the trucks left Ottawa, the CBC further reported that the Bitcoin donations continued to evade police. "Authorities are believed to be monitoring the remaining bitcoins but it remains unclear if they will be successful in capturing them," the report said.

"In order to have true freedom of expression," Caribou says, "we require money that cannot be manipulated, confiscated, or censored by the government. Bitcoin enables that freedom of expression, and we gave the world a playbook. It wasn't perfect. The option we went with in the end, with the envelopes, was the least crappy option that we could come up with in a bad situation. We created Version 1.0, and we documented it, and now the world has it."

Three months after the demonstration, Jeff Booth flew to Norway to speak to an annual human-rights conference, the Oslo Freedom Forum. Afterward, a woman approached him. "What you did saved countless lives," she said. She was Lyudmyla Kozlovska, the Ukrainian-born founder and president of the Open Dialogue Foundation, a human-rights organization administered from Poland and also from Belgium, where she now lives. When Russia invaded Ukraine on February 20, the day after police mopped up in Ottawa, Ukrainian authorities feared their banking system might collapse in the event of an all-out war. The Open Dialogue Foundation took the Bitcoin fundraising protocols developed for the Freedom Convoy — "Version 1.0" — and "in a few hours" raised enough Bitcoin to distribute, on the second day of the war, 100 bullet-proof vests, 100 helmets, and hundreds of medical kits to Ukrainian defence forces. Other Ukrainian NGOs followed the same example, Kozlovska says.

History is likely to record the Freedom Convoy Bitcoin campaign as the first demonstration of Bitcoin's ability to elude political and police repression. Specifically, history will record that Bitcoin registered its first anti-authoritarian success in Justin Trudeau's Canada.

Chapter 31

Illuminating the Darkness

What an irony. We initiated the Freedom Convoy to protest government overreach, and to shut us down the government overreached. After the police crackdown, the House of Commons resumed debate on the Emergencies Act. It was still in effect but Parliament had yet to vote its approval. Ya'ara Saks, Liberal member for the Toronto riding of York Centre and a duel Canadian-Israeli citizen, made an emotional case for why the protest had to be crushed. Having been fooled by a prank she saw online, she equated "honk, honk" with "H.H." and Nazi support among the truckers.

"How many guns need to be seized?" she asked rhetorically. "How much vitriol do we have to see of 'honk, honk,' which is an acronym for Heil Hitler?"

Ultimately, the House of Commons voted 185 to 151 in favour of Trudeau's use of the Emergencies Act. The New Democratic Party supported the Liberals, with erstwhile Trudeau critic Joël Lightbound voting with his own party. The Conservatives and Bloc Quebecois voted against. Two days later, when the Senate appeared reluctant to support the motion, Trudeau said he didn't need the act anymore anyway and revoked it. "Today, after careful consideration, we're ready to confirm that the situation is no longer an emergency," he said. "Therefore, the federal government will be ending the use of the Emergencies Act."

The act stipulates that if it is used, a judicial inquiry must follow. The idea is to determine whether the government used the act appropriately. An inquiry named the Public Order Emergency Commission was announced for the fall. In the meantime, a special Parliamentary joint committee began its own review. Seven MPs and four senators summoned witnesses to answer questions, and almost immediately a key government deception was exposed. Early and often, Public Safety Minister Marco Mendicino had been saying that the government invoked the Emergencies Act because the police asked them to. The joint committee revealed the statement to be a lie. At first, Mendicino had been stating it vaguely, then had grown increasingly more precise.

February 21, Question Period, after the act was invoked: "We continue to listen very carefully to the advice we are getting from our police services, which say that the Emergencies Act was instrumental in addressing the blockades at ports of entry and continues to be instrumental in preventing them."

February 25, Public Safety Committee: "That was the advice that we were receiving from law enforcement and one of the main reasons we invoked the Emergencies Act."

February 28, Question Period: "We had to invoke the Emergencies Act, and we did so on the basis of non-partisan professional advice from law enforcement."

March 1, Question Period: "We did invoke the Emergencies Act, but we did so as a last resort and on the advice of the police."

April 26, Joint Committee: "As we took our decision in what we could do to respond, we were following the advice of various levels of law enforcement, including the RCMP." At the same session, he said: "I don't want to speak for every last serving member of law enforcement, but there was a very strong consensus that we needed to invoke the act."

April 28, Question Period: "It was on the advice of law enforcement that we invoked the Emergencies Act."

May 3, Question Period: "We invoked the Emergencies Act on advice from police."

Every law enforcement official to appear before the Parliamentary joint committee, however, testified that they did not ask the government to invoke the act.

"No, there was never a question of requesting the Emergencies Act," RCMP Commissioner Brenda Lucki said. "I did not make that request," former Ottawa Police Chief Peter Sloly said, "[and] I'm not aware of anybody else in the Ottawa Police Service who did." Acting Ottawa chief Bell said the same. Similarly, Emergency Preparedness Minister Bill Blair told the committee he had heard of no police request. "I'm not aware of any recommendation of law enforcement," he said. "Quite frankly, this is a decision of government." Deputy Prime Minister Chrystia Freeland dodged the question saying, "I would like to take personal responsibility for that decision."

Usually, when a minister is found to have lied to Parliament, the minister is removed from cabinet, but Mendicino stayed. His deputy minister said Mendicino had been "misunderstood." Trudeau couldn't very well fire him, anyway, because the prime minister had presented the same justification to Parliament himself.

"Police were clear that they needed tools not held by any federal, provincial, or territorial law," Trudeau told Question Period on April 27. "It was only after we got advice from law enforcement that we invoked the Emergencies Act."

At the outset, Trudeau also said he would not involve the military. The *Globe and Mail*, however, despite its heavily biased coverage against the demonstrators, raised questions about a military presence. In April, two months after the crackdown, reporter Steven Chase wrote that a military spy plane had been circling the demonstration. His information came from Steffan Watkins, an Ottawa researcher who tracks ship and plane movements. On February 10, Day Thirteen of the protest, Watkins tracked a U.S.-registered King Air small passenger plane, with tail number N330TT. He recorded at least fifteen "precise and repeated" circles consistent with intelligence, surveillance and reconnaissance, or ISR, missions. "These patterns look very much like other tracks seen over foreign conflict zones while ISR missions were believed to be under way," Watkins told the *Globe*.

At the time, the Canadian military was awaiting delivery of three ISR aircraft, packed with surveillance gear, the paper said. The flight above Ottawa appeared to be training for the new planes. The *Ottawa Citizen* added to the story, quoting Watkins as saying he tracked the King Air over Ottawa on January 28 and 29, and on February 3, 10, and 11. The equipment onboard would have allowed Canadian special forces to intercept cellphone calls, radio transmissions, and other communications. Electro-optical sensors would also have allowed monitoring crews to track the movement of individuals and vehicles on the ground. The revelations appeared to give new meaning to Freeland's statement from before the police crackdown, "We can see what is happening and what is being planned in real time."

At first, the Department of National Defence would not acknowledge that the aircraft was working for the military. Later, pressed by the *Globe*, the department allowed that the flights were part of a military training operation for Canadian special forces. Asked specifically about the February 10 flight, Daniel Le Bouthillier, head of media relations at the defence department, said: "The flight in question was part of a Canadian Armed Forces training exercise that was planned prior to, and was unrelated to, the domestic event that was taking place at the time. This training had nothing to do with the surveillance or the monitoring of activities."

Watkins, on the other hand, pointed out that for regular training the aircraft could have flown anywhere in the Ottawa region, but the plane circled in specific flight patterns. "I believe their precise circular tracks over Ottawa suggest a form of electronic surveillance, not simply digital electro-optical imagery or video," Watkins said in a separate report on the flights and quoted in the *Ottawa Citizen* story.

In Question Period, Conservative MP Cheryl Gallant confronted the prime minister. "The government insists it did not deploy the military during the February demonstrations in Ottawa," she said. "Now we know surveillance flights were conducted over Ottawa at that time.... [W]as the surveillance conducted without lawful authority?"

"Mr. Speaker, here are the facts," Trudeau replied. "The flight in question was part of a Canadian Armed Forces training exercise that was planned prior to and was unrelated to the convoy protest. That is the fact."

Trudeau's response to the Freedom Convoy has permanently stained his record. He and Freeland exposed themselves to the world as autocrats, demanding of Canadians strict obedience to government mandates and displaying a stubborn unwillingness to compromise, or even to send somebody to talk to the demonstrators. I don't expect the government ever to tell the truth about what happened. I don't need it to. I was there. I witnessed the extraordinary national, cultural phenomenon for myself. For two years, honest working people remained quiet and civic-minded, doing their best to follow rules that the government said would bring the COVID-19 pandemic under control. When the rules turned illogical and overreaching — demanding that long-haul truckers take three molecular tests in a row and quarantine for two weeks no matter what the test results — people came together to call the government to account. They rose not in anger but in a festive spirit, with an exuberance accentuated by the chugging engines, the shining chrome, and the honking horns. In a show of good-natured unity, they broke the silence. They shattered the trance. No spike in COVID-19 cases resulted. No hospitals got overwhelmed. The political landscape, however, shifted.

The Conservative Party ousted its leader and a few months later elected Pierre Poilievre, a supporter of the truckers and of non-violent political protest. The truckers won a voice in the House of Commons. Provincial premiers relaxed their COVID-19 restrictions. Francois Legault withdrew his plan for a special tax on the unvaccinated. Scott Moe called out the ridiculousness of dividing the vaccinated and unvaccinated, and other premiers made other adjustments. Inspired by the Freedom Convoy, people in thirty countries, flying Canadian flags, held their own rallies and protests against similar growing infringements on personal freedoms. The Bitcoin network helped prove the need for a decentralized currency independent of governments and banks.

Above all other achievements of the Freedom Convoy, Canadian truckers and their supporters for three weeks, day after day, kept their protest non-violent. Nobody died. Nobody was injured except by the police. More problems have been seen at a single Rolling Stones concert than in Ottawa during the entire convoy demonstration. Essentially, everybody really did remain calm and loving toward each other. They made new friends, and many now count the convoy experience as a highlight of their life. In the months that followed, all summer long, convoy participants reunited in their respective regions for picnics, barbeques, mini-convoys, and camping weekends.

The question now is how to move forward. How do we perpetuate the spirit of determination, creativity, national pride, and togetherness that demonstrators shared during the Freedom Convoy? Everybody who attended has a story. One that stands out for me comes from Michael Grandlouis in a YouTube video he made two months after the police crackdown. Using his photos and video clips from the demonstration, he put together a two-part, eighty-minute documentary that includes one particularly powerful mental image.

Grandlouis is a member of the Wolf Lake (Algonquin) Nation near Temiskaming, at the Quebec-Ontario border. He lives in a downtown Ottawa condominium near Parliament Hill, close to what was the protest's epicentre. When the Ontario trucks started arriving on the first Friday, he walked out to see them. He was excited by the packed streets and loud horns, and saw restaurant owners handing out free sandwiches and wraps to welcome the truckers. "I started waving to people and everyone was waving back," he says in the documentary in his effusive way.

The next day, Saturday, Day One, he bundled up. The wind-chill reading hit minus thirty. He saw people walking — "purposefully," he says — toward Parliament Hill. Trucks were neatly stacked one behind the other all down Wellington Street. He walked between the rows, taking in the grease and diesel smells, which reminded him of the farm equipment he had known as a child. He turned and walked to the Alexandra Bridge, as we had that day, to watch the crowds coming across. After warming up at lunch he went out again. He walked to the National War Museum, to where Brigitte Belton had taken the Ontario convoys, and noticed trucks lined tip-to-tail beyond the museum along the Sir John A. Macdonald Parkway. He decided to greet every trucker in every rig. He walked from vehicle to vehicle, welcoming every driver, or couple, or family to his city. He met people from every part of Ontario, as far away as Kenora. He met people from Alberta and British Columbia, and from Nova Scotia and Newfoundland. At first, his idea was to walk to the end of the first rise, but when he got there he saw more trucks lined to the next rise, and more again to yet a more distant rise. He kept going, pausing at every truck to say hello. Finally, he reached the Island Park Bridge, six kilometres from Parliament Hill. Beyond that point, police had prevented trucks from parking.

By then, Grandlouis's face was so cold he could hardly talk anymore. "I was trying to be welcoming but I could barely open my mouth," he says. He had been walking for three hours. His beard was frozen. His ears were ringing from the horns. Near the bridge, a trucker from Manitoba and his wife offered to grill him a hamburger. Grandlouis was touched. No stranger had ever offered to cook him a hamburger before. Already, the meat was cooking on a hibachi. The man's wife asked what he'd like on it and, in the warmth of the cab, added condiments to a bun, then brought the bun out when the hamburger was ready. "I'd never seen that done before," Grandlouis says, delighted. "Good idea, right?"

After he finished eating, he started back downtown. In Ottawa, January is the darkest month. The sun sets early, and there were no street lamps along the parkway to light the way.

"I start walking back and I mean it's pitch black," Grandlouis says. He falters, getting emotional. "And this happened. So every eight or ten trucks, it's pitch black, they would just turn on their lights for me while I walked, and, when I would get out of sight, another truck would turn on its lights just to illuminate my path. And they did that the whole way."

For me, Grandlouis's story holds a lesson for everybody who wants to stay in the spirit of the Freedom Convoy, whether they were in Ottawa or not. As we go forward, sometimes we might want to turn on the headlights, lighting the way for others to walk ahead. At other times, we might want to be the one walking alone into darkness, letting others illuminate our path.

Acknowledgements

In the course of researching and writing the book, we received help from many people. Some are acknowledged in the text. Others deserve special thanks. Throughout the demonstration, Jordan Peterson made himself available on the phone, never presuming to give advice and always listening in a caring, supportive way. Diana Davison offered sound warnings and good strategic advice. Joseph Neuberger, Chris Assie, and Daniel Fairheight provided essential legal guidance. Jim Karahalios, leader of the New Blue Party of Ontario and a lawyer, acted as Benjamin's legal counsel at the Public Order Emergency Commission, the judicial inquiry into Trudeau's use of the Emergencies Act Donna Laframboise, author of the blog "Thank You, Truckers!," contributed indispensable editorial assistance. Three other readers — Ronald Albertson, Jamie Craig, and Phil Schockaert — clarified and improved the text. Alan Dean provided special support and good company, as did Melissa. Deb McKeen twice turned over her house to use as an editing retreat.

Benjamin also thanks: Charlie Serfaty for his inspiring life lessons about strength and never playing the victim; Mike, Jaco, and the boys for their help in Medellin when I could barely walk; Aedan, Aytan, Reviv, and Caroline for their support and friendship; Eric Goddard for his interest and support; Robyn, who knows how valuable she has been; the thousands of people in the global Bitcoin community who rallied to support the Canadian truckers' fight for freedom and those who congratulated the Freedom Convoy at Bitcoin Miami; the YouTube streamers who got out the truth; U.S. trucker and freelancer Gord Magill for writing about the Canadian truckers for his American audience; "DJ" for adding to my Twitter Spaces in his always informative way; Samantha Ottimo for preparing me for my first big interview on Tucker Carlson Tonight; Alex, Guy, Sean, Tomer, and the team at Swan Bitcoin who repeatedly invited me to talk about freedom in their Twitter Spaces; Bitcoin Magazine for their convoy coverage and for inviting me on their podcasts and Twitter Spaces; Ben from the YouTube channel BTC Sessions for tutorials that taught me everything I know about using Bitcoin and changed my life; Eduardo and his staff at the Second Cup, on Toronto's Danforth, for their friendly service at our weekly meetings; and my mother and father for teaching me the importance of positivity and love and the importance of never being afraid to fight when it truly matters.

Thank you especially to the thousands of American truckers who flew Canadian flags in solidarity with the Freedom Convoy. Most of all, thank you, my fellow Canadian truckers!